GROWING HOPE

GROWING HOPE

Daily Readings

Neil Paynter

WILD GOOSE PUBLICATIONS

Contents of book © the individual contributors
Compilation © 2006 Neil Paynter

First published 2006 by
Wild Goose Publications,
4th Floor, Savoy House, 140 Sauchiehall St, Glasgow G2 3DH, UK.
Wild Goose Publications is the publishing division of the Iona Community.
Scottish Charity No. SCO03794. Limited Company Reg. No. SCO96243.
www.ionabooks.com

ISBN 1-901557-99-5
13-digit ISBN: 978-1-901557-99-2

Cover illustration © The Iona Community

A catalogue record for this book is available from the British Library.

Overseas distribution:
Australia: Willow Connection Pty Ltd, Unit 4A, 3-9 Kenneth Road,
Manly Vale, NSW 2093
New Zealand: Pleroma, Higginson Street, Otane 4170, Central Hawkes Bay
Canada: Novalis/Bayard Publishing & Distribution, 10 Lower Spadina Ave.,
Suite 400, Toronto, Ontario M5V 2Z2

Permission to reproduce any part of this work in Australia or New Zealand
should be sought from Willow Connection.

Printed by Bell & Bain, Thornliebank, Glasgow

Coming here one day changed my whole life.

A volunteer with the Iona Community

To Dorothy

INTRODUCTION

This book grew out of a call to Iona Community members to send in their favourite quotes – quotes that have influenced and inspired them, quotes they have copied down in notebooks and diaries, quotes they have taken with them on demonstrations and rallies, quotes they have carried around in their minds, in their hearts ...

Not every quote I received for *Growing Hope* made the book, unfortunately. I am sorry about that. Many did. I had to make choices (an editor's responsibility and privilege). In the end, I had to make it 'easy' for myself and choose material I could source and which our budget could afford. There was lot of 'work and worship' involved, a lot of digging and praying. Still, it was a work of love.

Thank you to everyone who took the time and trouble to send me quotes; and thank you to everyone who gave permission for quotes to be included. Many contributors e-mailed me back almost immediately to give their go-ahead, happy and honoured to be part of a project supporting the Iona Community and the Growing Hope Appeal. If I have failed to obtain permission from anyone I hope they will forgive me; I have tried my best. Thanks also to Sandra Kramer, Tri Boi Ta, Alex O'Neill, Jane Riley and Suet-Lin Teo at Wild Goose Publications – you are amazing.

Growing Hope is not a comprehensive book detailing the influences and inspirations of the Iona Community. If I put out another call I would receive different quotes, and some of the same quotes no doubt. There are many writers and thinkers not included here who I know could be – theologians like Walter Wink and Gustavo Gutierrez, poets like Whitman and Ben Okri ... Still this book does express, to a good extent I think, and in a scattered, rich way, the concerns and spirit of the Iona Community. It is also, of course, a book about hope; hope runs through it. In a time when George Bush and Tony Blair are sowing and reaping the weeds of war, people around the world are being uprooted and scattered by governments, death squads and multi-national corporations, and climate change is creating chaos, we need hope.

Growing Hope is a book for daily reflection and meditation. A book to keep in your handbag or your briefcase. A book to keep on your bedside table or to read on the train in to work. A book to read in spare moments, and a book to read in the thick of it. Some readings are a sentence or two, others are a few paragraphs. They are short and to the point. Short and to the point because, it seems, that brevity and compactness is what the modern person has space and time for, but also because there is little time left, I feel – unless we act.

I hope this book gives you comfort but doesn't make you feel cosy. I hope it deepens your connection to the world in some way. May these little readings be seeds of hope; may they fall on good ground; may they sink in and take root in you.

'Hope comes from the grass roots,' somebody said. Hope comes from you and me, from everyday folk working in their communities. There are so many amazing, wonderful, committed people working to make this world a better place – I meet them all the time, working in nursing homes, working in youth clubs, working with children, working for nuclear disarmament, working in the environmental movement, working … It gives me hope.

Let's get it together; let's *get* together. Let's wrest this world away from the politicians and 'the money boys', as George MacLeod named them. I don't know about you, but I am no longer interested in building walls of security and privilege, in withdrawing into shopping, drugs, virtual reality … I no longer believe the lies: We are not alone. We are one body. We are in community. We are all connected on this precious, fragile, miracle of a planet.

We are not powerless. We have enormous potential power – let's use it. Let's scare the life out of the powers that be. Let's turn the tables. 'Never doubt,' wrote Margaret Mead (see the reading for July 21). Never doubt. Hope.

This book owes something to the booklets Peter and Dorothy Millar produced to help fund charitable projects in South India, where they worked for many years (*Prayers from a Columban House, Notes for a Pilgrim, Seeds of Hope*). If you like this book you will probably profit from their beautiful booklets. These are available from the Iona Community Shop on the isle of Iona (write to: The Iona Community's Shop, Isle of Iona, Argyll PA76 6SN). If you would like to read Dorothy and Peter's booklets, travel to Iona; they are there in the south aisle chapel of Iona Abbey, a deeply prayerful place, full of light and warmth and God's energy. Go to Iona, read a quote, light a candle … Read the quotes in this book each day and light a candle. Pray for the concerns suggested by the readings; pray for yourself and those close to you; think about ways to act in your community, in the wider world. Go out and make some difference; help to make hope grow. Be a candle. Be a seed. There is no other reason for you to be here on Earth really. Is there? What are we waiting for? What are we so frightened of? God is with us. 'Let your light shine,' said Jesus.

Camas and Iona are places of light. Crossroads where pilgrims from around the world – from Pakistan and Pollokshaws, from Uganda and Somerset – meet to share ideas, experiences, food, music, stories, late night talks and early morning worship; where folk learn to work together and to play again; where people can recharge, be accepted for who they are, gain understanding and strength and go out again on their journeys. The world desperately needs places like Camas and Iona; places where hope grows and spreads out – places where people can experience hope, love, trust, freedom …

The 'slogan' of the Growing Hope Appeal is 'Hope, Friends, Love, Trust, Freedom'. It's a good 'slogan' in this world of 24-hour commercials, ads, jingles … It's certainly a much better 'slogan' than 'Four More Years!', or 'Whoever has the most toys wins', or 'It's not racist to impose limits on immigration. Are You Thinking What We're Thinking?' (the Conservative Party, 2005) …

'Hope, Friends, Love, Trust, Freedom'– don't you wish a political party would run on that platform? I'd certainly vote for them. Or is that naïve, to believe in love, hope, friends, trust, freedom in this complicated time, dark age?

O God, help my unbelief.
Help me to believe in love,
hope,
friends
love,
trust,
freedom:

Hope in the future,
Friends who affirm and challenge and inspire us,
Love as the guiding force of the universe,
Trust between peoples and nations,
Freedom from suffering for the world's oppressed and marginalised people.
O God, make me your child.

Neil Paynter
Biggar, Scotland,
Advent 2005

January

January 1

NEW WAYS

God of our lives,
you are always calling us
to follow you into the future,
inviting us to new ventures, new challenges,
new ways to care,
new ways to touch the hearts of all.
When we are fearful of the unknown, give us courage.
When we worry that we are not up to the task,
remind us that you would not call us
if you did not believe in us.

When we get tired,
or feel disappointed with the way things are going,
remind us that you can bring change and hope
out of the most difficult situations.

Kathy Galloway, a member of the Iona Community

Leader: This is the day that God has made;
ALL: WE WILL REJOICE AND BE GLAD IN IT.

Leader: We will not offer to God
ALL: OFFERINGS THAT COST US NOTHING.

Leader: Go in peace to love and to serve;
ALL: WE WILL SEEK PEACE AND PURSUE IT.

Leader: In the name of the trinity of love,
ALL: GOD IN COMMUNITY, HOLY AND ONE.

Responses used in Iona Abbey

To walk in the light is to walk freely not fearfully, to see and delight in all the beauty around us: in people, in nature, desiring it to be allowed to remain beautiful. It is to walk with a light heart, relaxed not tense, to have choices. The light is in the world. There is an old Jewish saying, 'Do not say, God is in my heart. Rather, say, I am in the heart of God.' The gospel of Jesus says precisely this thing. I am in God's heart, and you, and you and you. Loved, valued, unconditionally accepted, we live and move and have our being in the heart of God, which is the light of God.

Kathy Galloway

Follow the light you have
and pray for more light.

George MacLeod, founder of the Iona Community

NOW

The reawakening to mystery is leading us to an attentiveness to the present moment ... This moment that we're given is, in itself, a precious moment, and we ourselves are precious within it.

Peter Millar, a member of the Iona Community, from a sermon

Living with cancer

Thank you for giving me a wake-up call:
to look at the world with new eyes,
to live NOW –
not stuck in the past,
not fretting away for an unknown and unknowable future.
Thank you for giving me the chance to look at life afresh.

I know to trust you and not to worry:
to live fully and value each precious moment,
to cherish each part of your creation,
to seek you in each person I meet,
to live with joy,
which I have too often denied.

Thank you for blessing me.

Zam Walker Coleman, a member of the Iona Community

To become aware of the sacramental nature of the cosmos,
to be open to the sacramental possibilities of each moment,
to see the face of Christ in every person –
these things are not novel,
but their rediscovery is the beginning of our health.

Ron Ferguson, a member of the Iona Community

Spirituality is what makes you get out of bed in the morning.

Kathy Galloway

A PRAYER FOR THIS DAY

God of the dawning, grant me hope for this day
that I may walk in your pathway and live in your light.

God of the morning, grant me purpose to go forward
to respond to the promise of opportunities to love and serve.

God of the noontide, grant me strength as I labour to serve,
to keep my head high, and fulfil my commitment to the task.

God of the rest-hour, grant me grace to be still,
to know the healing balm of time alone, and to find you in the peace.

God of the evening, grant me space and time
to let go of my responsibilities,
to enjoy the pleasures of rest and the company of those I love.

God of the night, grant me the faith to face the darkness without fear,
to know that you will hold me in the blessed sleep of time and eternity.

God of all my days, grant me the promise of days yet to come,
and the thankfulness of past days well used.

Tom Gordon, a member of the Iona Community

January 5

ACKNOWLEDGING OUR FRAGILITY

Just after the Christmas and New Year holidays it occurred to me that the only organisation that met during the holidays in the church was Alcoholics Anonymous. It was the only organisation crucial enough for its members that it had to keep going over the holidays. Obviously that said something about A.A., but it also says something about the church. What were the lessons?

Alcoholics Anonymous is not only a community of the fragile, it is a community whose members, day by day, week by week, acknowledge their fragility; they remind themselves and each other of how fragile they are. Not so the church. You may come to the church as a 'sinner', but you are expected to get 'better'. Your life is supposed to take on shape, and substance, and a kind of certainty. If 'your faith' cannot sustain you through anxiety, illness or bereavement, then that's seen as a judgement on your faith; your faith is flawed. If the church member who was once perhaps a boozer goes back on the booze, what does the church say? 'Shame, shame, terrible, terrible!' If you are a church member you are supposed to be a coping sort of person.

Are we not too respectable, are we also too secure? Too respectable and secure to have much hope of having ears that hear the expected word of grace, or eyes that see the unexpected vision of grace. Are we too respectable, too secure?

Are we? I wonder.

Or are we not perhaps much more like the alcoholic who will not admit his alcoholism? The alcoholic who says, 'Who me? I've nae drink problem … look at these hands, steady as a rock,' even if he's bevvied out his mind at the time of speaking. Are we not conditioned in the Kirk to wear a facade of certainty and respectability, however fragile and uncertain a heart beats within us? Has the church not conditioned us to think that it's somehow improper to show our insecurity? How can we ever become the kind of community that brings life where there is death – and make no mistake, the faith is about something as dramatic as that – how can we be that kind of community if we are conditioned, for whatever reasons the church may have had, if we are conditioned to hide the death and decay of our living?

Erik Cramb, a member of the Iona Community

Prayer

O God,
help us to admit our fragility
and to be gentle with each other.

Neil Paynter

January 6

EPIPHANY

If you are going on pilgrimage to find Christ, you will only find him if you carry him in your heart.

Irish monastic saying

Let your feet follow your heart until you find your place of resurrection.

Celtic Christian saying

Blessing

Bless O God,
the journey ahead.
Bless the travelling
and the arrival.
Bless those who welcome
and those who accept hospitality,
that Christ may come among us
in journeying and in stillness.

Kate McIlhagga, a member of the Iona Community

January 7

INTO THE THICK OF THINGS

Our hearts are set on pilgrim roads not to satisfy ourselves with finding one holy place, not to romanticise this thin place, but to take the experience of the presence of the Holy back into the thick of things. When our hearts are set on pilgrim roads, we can come to know God's spirit who permeates 'every blessed thing' and every blessed body; when our hearts are set on pilgrimage roads we struggle to find the HOLY where we are – in the ordinary cities and towns where we live, in this world where, as the Peruvian poet says, 'suffering and death increase sixty minutes in every second'. The life of discipleship brings us to see and know the face of Jesus in his most distressing guise: in the poor, the hungry, the stranger, the abused, the addict, the desperate and deranged, the elderly and the demented, the panhandlers and prostitutes, the criminal and the condemned. Because these are the friends of Jesus, the poor and the poor in spirit, the vulnerable, those who know their need for healing and cannot hide their vulnerability and desperation. When our eyes can see with pilgrim hearts through the thick grime and human wreckage we know with clarity and certainty that these – the least of our sisters and brothers – are those in whom Jesus Christ hides himself and invites us to recognise him and reach out in solidarity and love.

Murphy Davis, The Open Door Community, Atlanta, Georgia, after pilgrimage to Iona in 2002

January 8

A THREAD OF GOLD

A 19th-century teacher in Celtic tradition used the analogy of royal garments. In the 19th century royal garments were still woven through with a costly thread, a thread of gold. If somehow the golden thread were removed from the garment, the entire garment would unravel. So it is, he said, with the image of God woven into the fabric of our being. If somehow it were taken out of us, we would unravel, we would cease to be. The image of God is not simply a characteristic of who we are, which may or may not be there depending on whether or not we have received the grace of baptism. The image of God is the essence of our being, and sin has not had the power to undo what God has woven into the fabric of our being.

The belief that what is deepest in us is the image of God has a number of radically important implications for our spirituality. It is to say that the wisdom of God is deeper in our souls than the ignorance of what we have become. It is to say that the beauty of God is truer to our depths than the ugliness of what we have done. Similarly it is to say that the creativity of God and the passion of God for what is just and right is deeper than any barrenness or apathy in our lives. And above all else it is to say that love, the desire to love and the desire to be loved, is at the very centre of the mystery of our being, deeper than any fear or hatred that may hold us hostage.

This is not to be naïve about the power of sin and the perversion of what has gone wrong in our souls and relationships. It is simply to say that what God has planted at the core of our beings has not been undone by sin.

J Philip Newell, an associate member of the Iona Community and former warden of Iona Abbey

WE AFFIRM THAT WE ARE MADE IN GOD'S IMAGE,
BEFRIENDED BY CHRIST,
EMPOWERED BY THE SPIRIT.

From the affirmation of the morning service, Iona Abbey

January 9

REBORN

It is impossible to live and work among Muslims without being very aware of the five pillars of Islam, by which their lives are regulated, and to see their universal observance – people really do stop what they are doing to pray five times a day, they do fast at Ramadan, they do give alms if they are able, they do proclaim their faith once in their lifetime and they do all long to be able to make the Hajj (the pilgrimage to Mecca during the last month of the Muslim year).

Just before I left Qasmiyeh in 1994, my neighbour, Im Fahmi, a widow, and her unmarried daughter, Miriam, wanted to go to Mecca. It is forbidden for any unmarried woman to go unless with her brother. All Miriam's brothers are living in Germany so she was temporarily married 'on paper' to the uncle who was going to escort them. On the day of their departure they had to dress in the obligatory white garments and we all gathered to speed them on their way.

The Hajj is a real endurance test – millions of pilgrims, heat, dust and walking and walking. The travel and accommodation are carefully arranged and the pilgrims are housed together with fellow pilgrims from their country of origin, for, of course, they come from all over the world. Very wisely every pilgrim is issued with a wrist band on which the name and the hotel where they are staying is written, a wise precaution as Miriam unfortunately became separated from her mother but was later reunited. It was a miracle to me that Im Fahmi, who is in her sixties, survived and completed the whole of the Hajj … One of Im Fahmi's sons travelled specially from Germany to Qasmiyeh to prepare the welcome home for his mother and sister. He paved the entrance to their house, previously a muddy path, and erected an arch painted with congratulatory slogans decorated with flowers. They arrived home safely albeit exhausted, but renewed. The Hajj carries a most definite meaning – it is not a holiday, nor a picnic, it is not just a ritual and not only an obligation, it should be a profound spiritual experience. Im Fahmi and Miriam returned radiant, saying they had been through a process of purification and felt reborn and should never again say anything bad about other people.

Dr Runa Mackay, a member of the Iona Community

THE FRUITS OF LOVING

In the joy of conversations,
in the laughter of jokes,
in the risk of encountering personality,
in the fear of exposed vulnerability,
in the danger of loving,
in the unpredictability of all relationships,

in the midst of all of these,
we find strength for the way.
Affirmation of our humanity,
solace for our souls.
We glimpse the deep potentials of life,
the joy of growth, and the realisation of our identity.

For the way of love is at cost,
a way of pain, brutality, risk.
But a way which is of life and all its fullness.
A life which blossoms with the seed of our human potential.
The life we were meant to lead is found.

Scott Blythe, a member of the Iona Community

QURBANI

Eid-ul-Adha, the second Eid – marked this year by a great fire among the tents near Mecca. Over 300 deaths and about 1000 injured. The victims are mainly from India, Pakistan and Bangladesh. There is great concern among the Muslims here.

I visited several homes during this three-day festival. In one I arrived just as the housewife was busy sweeping the carpet clean after the departure of a family and their children. She uses a dustpan and a hand brush. Other visitors begin to arrive. Cups of tea and plates of sweetmeats are passed around.

A grandfather talks of his worry about his daughter, her husband and their children. They had lived in overcrowded conditions with her sister's family. Now they had been offered a council house some distance away. What would happen if there was trouble on the estate? What if there was an emergency, perhaps the children ill? Her husband worked in a restaurant in another town, too far away to come home except when he had a day off. His daughter needed some support. She needed a house near her family.

It was time to go. The housewife disappeared into the kitchen and emerged with a plastic box containing cooked rice and salad. 'Take this for yourself and your wife,' she said. At this festival a man came to our house with a parcel of about a pound of lamb. This, he explained, was part of Qurbani, the giving required at Eid-ul-Adha.

Stanley Hope, a member of the Iona Community

NEEDLE AND THREAD

I met an Irish woman in the market who told me that her daughter and husband had become Muslims. He had now ceased to drink after being a heavy drinker.

Stanley Hope, from an article

Prayer

O God, I am Mustafah the tailor and I work at the shop of Muhammad Ali. The whole day long I sit and pull the needle and the thread through the cloth. O God, you are the needle and I am the thread. I am attached to you and I follow you. When the thread tries to slip away from the needle it becomes tangled up and must be cut so that it can be put back in the right place. O God, help me to follow you wherever you may lead me. For I am really only Mustafah, the tailor, and I work at the shop of Muhammad Ali on the great square.

Prayer of a Muslim who had come to follow Christ

GOD, THANKS FOR WELCOMING ME AGAIN

God, thanks for welcoming me again.

I look into my heart, and I am not proud of what I see there. I look into my mind, and it is cluttered with worries and concerns and important business. I look at my hands, and they are full of the things I think I need for my comfort and security.

God, you welcome me before I am ready,
while I am still in a mess.
But you don't care about the mess.

You can see deeper into my heart, to the beauty and potential you have made there. You know what my mind will be like when I have learned how to stop being so serious and worried about life and work. You know what my hands will hold when I have learned how to empty them for you to fill.

You love me and you love each one of us with the same enthusiasm and hope. You know what we can be. Help us to empty our hearts and minds and hands of all that is unnecessary and teach us how to care for and welcome one another every day, with the same affection and generosity with which you welcome us.

From *The Iona Community Worship Book*

When we are happy
when we are full of fun and laughter
GOD WELCOMES US

When we are angry
When people let us down
GOD WELCOMES US

When we are tired
When we need to stop and curl up and rest
GOD WELCOMES US

God of welcome
God your door is always open
WE ARE GLAD TO MEET YOU HERE

Ruth Burgess, a member of the Iona Community

January 14

IN A NEW LIGHT

Whenever they wanted to escape from others, he made them stay with them and see them in a new light. When they wanted to send the mothers and children away, he took a child and said that this was the person they should follow. When they wanted him to send the crowd away so that they could enjoy a spiritual retreat, he made them feed the people. He attacked their love of isolation from all sides. They wanted to remain isolated from foreigners, strangers, women, children, outcasts. Their love of isolation had become for them a virtue. It had been built up by their education, their religious customs, their national pride. He led them into the world of other men, of all other men. For them isolation was at an end. And, in ending their isolation, they began to know Jesus.

Ralph Morton, a founding member of the Iona Community

READING FOR WORLD RELIGION DAY

Christians say: Do to others what you would have them do to you.
Jews say: What is hateful to you, do not to your fellow man.
Buddhists say: Hurt not others in ways that you yourself would find hurtful.
Muslims say: No one of you is a believer until he desires for his brother that which he desires for himself.
Sikhs say: Treat others as you would be treated yourself.
Hindus say: This is the sum of duty: Do not do to others what would cause pain if done to you.

Source unknown

BLESSED ARE THE PEACEMAKERS

I believed I was going to serve the human people, the Israelis and Arabs, because nuclear weapons can kill everyone.

Mordechai Vanunu, technician arrested in the 1980s for exposing that Israel possessed nuclear weapons

Doubtless you members of the jury would agree that sabotaging the ovens of Auschwitz would have been a moral duty. The movable incinerator that is Trident is many times more lethal.

Ellen Moxley, Trident Ploughshares 2000 defendant, and a member of the Iona Community (The UK's Trident nuclear submarine base is at Faslane, near Helensburgh, Scotland.)

Who brings about peace is called the companion of God in the work of creation.

Jewish saying

January 17

BEING YOURSELF

One of the favourite figures in early Celtic legend is the 3rd-century Christian contemplative, Antony of the Desert. He even appears etched into the designs of high-standing Celtic crosses. Antony was remembered as saying to those who came out to see him in his desert hermitage, 'When you die and go to your place of judgement, you will not be asked whether you have become another St Paul or St Mary. You will be asked whether you have become truly yourself.' In the Celtic tradition there is a passionate and rigorous emphasis on repentance. Repentance, however, which simply means turning around, is a turning around not to become someone other than ourselves. It is turning away from falseness of what we have become to re-turn to the true depths of our nature.

J. Philip Newell

Move among us, O God; give us life:
LET YOUR PEOPLE REJOICE IN YOU.

Responses from the morning service, Iona Abbey

HOPE FOR THE WORLD

Leader: In quietness and darkness,
in peace and confusion,
Jesus Christ wants to make his home
and meet his friends.
He is the light of life:

ALL: HE IS HOPE FOR THE WORLD.

Leader: In him there is neither Jew nor Gentile,
neither Roman Catholic nor Protestant,

ALL: ALL ARE ONE IN JESUS CHRIST.

Leader: He is the light of life:

ALL: HE IS HOPE FOR THE WORLD.

Leader: In him is neither black nor white,
neither north nor south:

ALL: ALL ARE ONE IN JESUS CHRIST.

Leader: He is the light of life:

ALL: HE IS HOPE FOR THE WORLD.

Leader: In him is neither male nor female,
neither master nor servant:

ALL: ALL ARE ONE IN JESUS CHRIST.

Leader: He is the light of life:

ALL: HE IS HOPE FOR THE WORLD.

Leader:	In him there is neither rich nor poor,
	neither middle class nor working class:
ALL:	ALL ARE ONE IN JESUS CHRIST.

| Leader: | He is the light of life: |
| ALL: | HE IS HOPE FOR THE WORLD. |

Wild Goose Resource Group

For Christ himself has brought us peace by making Jews and Gentiles one people. With his own body he broke down the wall that separated them and kept them enemies.

Ephesians 2:14 (GNB)

January 19

COURAGE TO HOPE

Hope has two beautiful daughters. Their names are Anger and Courage: Anger at the way things are, and Courage to see that they do not remain the way they are.

Attributed to St Augustine of Hippo

Prayer

God, give me once more the courage to hope.
Fertilise my barren mind.
Let me hope again.

Søren Kierkegaard

Strong and mysterious
Bright and holy
GOD IS ON THE SIDE OF LOVE

Wise and questioning
Just and joyful
GOD IS ON THE SIDE OF TRUTH

Wild and challenging
Glorious and graceful
GOD IS ON THE SIDE OF HOPE

Ruth Burgess, a member of the Iona Community

January 20
Martin Luther King Day

In our day of space vehicles and guided ballistic missiles, the choice is either nonviolence or nonexistence.

Martin Luther King

MLK Day was celebrated for the first time on January 20th, 1986.

AT THE END OF THIS DAY

I reflect on this day ...
giving thanks for all the gifts I have received in it:
for those ordinary gifts of every day which I so often take for granted;
for the special gifts of today –
anything which I have seen, or heard, or done or thought about today
which has given me pleasure;
for the unlooked-for gift –
that which has upset me or disturbed me or
stopped me in my tracks
but which I can learn from;
for those things which have made me aware of my need of God today.

I pause to reflect on what I ought to remember from today –
a word, an incident, a conversation, a feeling –
and ask myself,
what might God have been trying to teach me today?

Is there anything for which I need to be sorry,
and which I should bring before God's love and forgiveness?
Am I carrying any concern or anxiety that I can surrender to God's love tonight?

With what do I need help tomorrow?

In the stillness of the evening I pray
for light to guide me into tomorrow,
and for arms to hold me through the night.

Lynda Wright, a member of the Iona Community

As I dig for wild orchids
in the autumn fields,
it is the deeply bedded root
that I desire,
not the flower.

Izumi Shikibu, Japan (974–1034)

I thought that my voyage had come to its end at the last limit of my power – that the path before me was closed, that provisions were exhausted and the time come to take shelter in a silent obscurity. But I find that thy will knows no end in me. And when old words die out on the tongue, new melodies break forth from the heart; and where the old tracks are lost, new country is revealed with its wonders.

Rabindranath Tagore

THE SACRED DUTY OF HOSPITALITY

The idea is that when you share the 'cup of kindness' with a stranger, you may be sharing with none other than God. This is, of course, a very Christian idea (Matthew 10), but I know that similar principles are found at the root of Islamic, Hindu and Sikh hospitality.

Hospitality is, of course, for the short term. That's why, for the long haul, many societies that have a strong understanding of creating communities of place also have an ethic of fostership. This is certainly true of Scotland. Indeed, in Scottish culture there is a recognition that fostership, as a process of choosing and being chosen to belong to a place, counts for even more than blood lineage.

As the Gaelic proverb puts it, 'The bonds of milk (i.e. nurture) are stronger than the bonds of blood' (i.e. lineage). And as another popular saying has it, 'We're all Jock Tamson's bairns' – meaning that all the world's people come from one common ancestor (who, of course, has a commonplace Scottish name!).

Alastair McIntosh, a patron of the Growing Hope Appeal and an associate member of the Iona Community

January 25

CHANGING PLACES

Robert Burns famously wrote: 'Oh, wad some power the giftie gie us, tae see ourselves as ithers see us', and I guess it is this admirable hope (as well as the hope of better ratings, of course) that has driven the current plethora of 'changing places' reality television shows. Members of the great British public have swapped wives, houses, gardens, lifestyles, holiday venues, workplaces and tastes in interior décor, and, in the latest exchange, bosses. The results of all this activity are sometimes amusing, gently entertaining and curiously moving, sometimes queasy, embarrassing or downright disturbing ... But I can't help feeling that the most interesting swaps are the ones we never see, perhaps because they might raise too many questions, might disturb the status quo too much, and move the changing place experiences too far from being the 'bread and circuses' provision it essentially is. What might it look like for the relentlessly negative political commentator to change places with the local government politician responsible for a huge range of policy that directly affects the lives of ordinary people, and faced with competing and sometimes incompatible demands? How about swapping the editor of *The Daily Mail* with a Zimbabwean or Roma asylum seeker, or Charles Clarke with a student working two jobs and still piling up the debt, or Tony Blair with a citizen of Baghdad? How about exchanging Robert Kilroy Silk for an Egyptian doctor saving lives daily or a Palestinian journalist risking his life daily ... The possibilities are endless ...

Kathy Galloway

January 26

THE WRITING ON THE WALL

Born in poverty
died in custody
in an age of technology

Aboriginal graffiti on an office tower in downtown Brisbane, Australia

First they came for the Jews
and I did not speak out –
because I was not a Jew.

Then they came for the communists
and I did not speak out –
because I was not a communist.

Then they came for the trade unionists
and I did not speak out –
because I was not a trade unionist.

Then they came for me –
and there was no one left
to speak out for me.

Pastor Martin Niemoller, a victim of the Nazis

Prayer

Remember, Lord, not only the men and women of good will but also those of ill will. But do not only remember all the suffering they have inflicted on us, remember the fruits we brought forth, thanks to this suffering – our comrade-ship, our loyalty, our humility, the courage, the generosity, the greatness of heart which has grown out of all this.

And when they come to judgement let all the fruits that we have borne be their forgiveness.

Prayer found after the liberation of Ravensbrück concentration camp, author unknown

HOLY GROUND

'When I got to India, I discovered that God had been at home there for a very long time.'

George More, a member of the Iona Community who spent thirty years working in India.

'What a mistake we made when we first went to Nyasaland! We forgot that, of course, God had been there before us. So we set about preparing to introduce him like a foreign visitor.'

A C McAlpine (former UF missionary), to Fergus Macpherson

Our first task in approaching other people, another culture, another religion, is to take off our shoes, for the place we are approaching is holy. Else we may find ourselves treading on men's dreams. More serious still, we may forget God was there before our arrival.

Canon Max Warren, General Secretary of the Church Missionary Society

READING FOR HOMELESSNESS SUNDAY

Someday we shall dance

Murphy Brinkley lives in my backyard. His feet are twisted because, during much of his adult life, he has not possessed shoes that fit. He is sixty years old. When it rains, he gets wet. When the temperature falls, he does too. He is waiting for Jesus or Moses or Matubu, the African king of yore, to come and set him free from the horror of homelessness. In Murphy Brinkley I hear hope banging at my back door. He hasn't given up. He has not quit. Passion for life has not been taken from him. He loves my daughter, Hannah, and sends her off to school each morning with kindness and admonitions to 'pay attention and study hard'. He welcomes me in the midnight hour after I've listened to Luther 'Houserocker' Johnson pick his wild red guitar with his teeth. He laughs and teases, plays and prays in my backyard. Mr Brinkley was not meant to live this way. No one is. Even our ancestors found caves of hollows in the giant trees. He is dying. Homelessness is death, a quiet nonjudical death penalty that even Bill Clinton would not fly home to Arkansas to watch. I love Murphy Brinkley and he loves me. Someday we shall dance.

Foxes have holes
Birds have nests
The son of humanity
Has no place to lay his head.
Neither does John, Henry,
Blue, Rock, Willy, Beth, Jane, Kahil, Pete,
Malcolm, Kathy, 102340, EF 124884, Harold.

Ed Loring, The Open Door Community, Atlanta, Georgia

January 30

WHAT IS INVISIBLE

What is love if it remains invisible and intangible? 'Those who do not love a brother or sister whom they have seen cannot love God whom they have not seen.' (1 Jn 4:20). The devastating poverty in which millions of children live is visible. Racism is visible. Machine guns are visible. Slums are visible. Starved bodies are visible. The gap between the rich and the poor is glaringly visible. Our response to these realities must be visible. Grace cannot function in a world of invisibility.

Yet, in our world the rulers try to make invisible 'the alien, the orphan, and the widow' (Jer 7:6; see Ex 22:22, Ps 82:3, Mk 12:40, Jas 1:27), and the 'hungry, thirsty, stranger, naked, sick and imprisoned' (Matt 25:31–46). This is violence. The gospel insists on visibility – the emaciated bodies of starved children must remain visible to the world. There is a connection between invisibility and violence. People, because of the dignity of the image of God they embody, must remain seen. Faith, hope and love are not vital except in 'what is seen'. The ecumenical movement seeks the visible unity of the churches. Was not God visible in Jesus Christ (Jn 1:18, 14:9)? The gospel sees the mystery of salvation in what is seen. Religions seem to raise up the invisible and despise what is visible. But it is the 'hear, see, touch' gospel that can nurture the hope which is free from deception.

Kosuke Koyama, speaking at the World Council of Churches Assembly in Harare

Christ is the visible likeness of the invisible God.

Colossians 1:15 (GNB)

January 31

Light a candle, don't just curse the darkness.

A Chinese saying often used by Stanley Hope, a member of the Iona Community

February

February 1

What is to give light must endure burning.

Viktor Frankl

A dimly burning wick he will not quench; he will faithfully bring forth justice.

Isaiah 42:3 (NRSV)

February 2

God dwells among the lowliest of men. He sits on the dust-heap among the prison convicts. With the juvenile delinquents He stands at the door, begging bread. He throngs with the beggars at the place of alms, He is among the sick. He stands in line with the unemployed in front of the free employment bureaux.

Therefore, let him who would meet God visit the prison cell before going to the temple. Before he goes to the church let him visit the hospital. Before he reads his Bible let him help the beggar standing at his door.

If he visits the prison after going to the temple, does he not by so much delay his meeting with God? If he goes first to the church and then to the hospital, does he not by so much postpone beholding God? If he fails to help the beggar at his door and indulges himself in Bible-reading, there is a danger lest God, who lives among the mean, will go elsewhere. In truth he who forgets the unemployed forgets God.

Toyohiko Kagawa

JABBERING AWAY

A Catholic bishop at an interfaith conference was somewhat bemused when a leader of another faith said to him, 'I'm surprised when Christians say "Let us pray" and then they immediately jabber away, with not a bit of silence or reflection.'

Be still, and know that I am God!

Psalm 46:10 (NRSV)

A GLOBAL ETHIC

In order to unite with one another we must love one another;
in order to love one another, we must know one another;
in order to know one another, we must go and meet one another.

From the testament of Cardinal Mercier, Archbishop of Malines-Brussels, 1926

No peace among the nations without peace among the religions.
No peace among the religions without dialogue between the religions.
No dialogue between the religions without investigation of the foundation of the religions.

Hans Küng

February 5

FAITH, HOPE AND CHARITY

Christian beliefs and values do not stem from social utopian thinking ... They are practical. Faith, hope and charity are their working tools in situations where many feel that a rich society, living on tax cuts, has negated the moral responsibilities that would alleviate the growing deprivation of the poor.

Larry Nugent, a member of the Iona Community

Prayer

As tools come to be sharpened by the blacksmith,
so may we come, Lord.

As sharpened tools go back with their owner,
so may we go back to our everyday life to be used by you.

A prayer from Africa

February 6

To clasp our hands in prayer is the beginning of an uprising against the order of the world.

Karl Barth

PRAYER OF RUSSIAN CHRISTIANS

Forgive us all.
Bless us all:
The thieves and the Samaritans,
Those that fall by the wayside
And the priests who pass by without stopping;
All our neighbours,
The villains and the victims,
The cursing and the cursed,
Those who rebel against you
And those who abandon themselves to your love.
Take us all
Into you,
Holy and just God.

Translated from the French by Rosemary Power, a member of the Iona Community

PRAYER

Christ of the pilgrim path,
and of every pilgrim heart,
thank you for revealing yourself
in situations we would prefer
to pass by.

Peter Millar, a member of the Iona Community

February 9

A WELCOMING BLESSING

May you meet God
in every place, in every person
and in the depths of your own heart.

Jan Sutch Pickard, a member of the Iona Community

February 10

A GARLAND OF FLOWERS

They arrived in two cars soon after 10:00 pm. They had just come from Manchester airport where they had been to welcome the wife of a young man in the party. His mother said she wanted our home to be the first place the young wife visited because I had helped in getting the documents together for the interview for a visa in Pakistan. The couple had been married in Pakistan six months earlier.

They crowd into the room. Everyone talks at once. The young wife looks tired after the long flight and the journey from the airport. She seems bewildered and shy as she looks round the ring of strange faces. She wears a garland of flowers. I notice on the palms of her hands an intricate pattern in henna. After ten minutes they pile into the two cars and leave.

Four days later I am invited to tea at the home of her mother-in-law where she is staying. Before the meal I had an opportunity to talk with her in Urdu. The conversation was the usual polite first meeting. We ask about each other's families. She tells me about her parents and her brothers and her sisters. She asks about my wife, myself and our two sons. She has spent most of her life in Karachi but as a child she lived in Bahrain. But soon she says how shaken and surprised she was by the many questions asked at the British High Commission when interviewed for a visa.

Soon the neighbours begin to arrive. Young and old, more women than men, all coming to welcome her to this strange land. This would continue for several days.

Stanley Hope, a member of the Iona Community

Treat them as you would a fellow-Israelite, and love them as you love yourselves. Remember that you were once foreigners in the land of Egypt. I am the Lord your God.

Leviticus 19:34 (GNB)

February 11

When elephants fight, the grass suffers.

Old African saying

The only way to eat an elephant is in small pieces.

Old African saying, used by Archbishop Desmond Tutu

February 12

EDUCATION

Education is as much a cradling of the soul as it is a feeding of the mind.

Ewan Aitken, a member of the Iona Community

Our task is to help young people experience the sheer delight of being alive.

Rev. Geoff Shaw, first leader of Strathclyde Regional Council and a member of the Gorbals Group

February 13

'Do something useful every day and don't get found out.'

Tubby Clayton, Toc H

February 14
St Valentine's Day

The beginning of love is to let those we love be perfectly themselves, and not to twist them to fit our own image. Otherwise we love only the reflection of ourselves we find in them.

Thomas Merton

Love is our awareness of God's coming in someone else.

Ralph Morton, a founding member of the Iona Community

It is only with the eyes of love that we'll see His coming.

Ralph Morton

A SEEDBED OF FAITH AND HOPE

Drumchapel is one of Glasgow's housing schemes. Much of the place is being 'regenerated': original, damp, shabby housing is being replaced or 'spruced up'. But even transformed housing doesn't necessarily transform people. Poverty and injustice is all around, not only material poverty but even worse – the poverty of lack of self-worth: 'I'm scum' – the words of a young mother still ring in my ears. She believed what other people said about her out of ignorance or a need to control. My heart aches every time I hear words like that; is it any wonder some people turn to substance abuse and self-harming? My heart heals again each time I see someone grow in confidence. Our local churches' family project, 3D Drumchapel, makes a deal of difference in the lives of a few families and young people; our congregation does too – and we're not alone. Drum-chapel is a seedbed of faith and hope.

I learn much from people here; probably the most important thing is that hope is not just about looking on the bright side; it is about being involved in the heartache of all that is wrong in the world and being a part of its transformation …

Carolyn Smyth, a member of the Iona Community and local URC minister

Hope is no half-hearted holy optimism about the far future.
It is not sentimental sloganising like
'Always look on the bright side of life.'
Hope is not an expectation or an anticipation
that we will live to see the results of our labours.
The seed never sees the flower …

Brian Quail, a member of the Iona Community, from 'Resistance and Hope Rap'

February 17

A COMMUNITY WHICH DANCES

A community which dances is a community of spirit, which knows the need to affirm the connections between self and larger reality; which knows the need to create spaces of energy, passion and delight, in the midst of hardship, pain or tedium; which knows that struggles for survival and justice will be afflicted by rigor mortis if not enlivened by the breath of celebration. I am with Emma Goldman and Rosa Luxembourg – it's not my revolution if I can't dance to it.

Lesley Orr, a member of the Iona Community

When we pray, we move our feet

African proverb

My body is like a rabah*
My heart is like a tambourine
Rhythm throbs in my veins
Every hair on my body
Sings one note
And that note is your name, God

Amir Khusro Dehlavi (1253–1325), Sufi mystic

* A type of stringed instrument

THE SEVENTH WAR FROM NOW

I am reminded of the story of a Vietnam protester who sat on the pavement holding a poster. When he was asked what he was trying to do he replied: 'I am trying to stop the seventh war from now.'

Roger Gray, a member of the Iona Community

Far too few Christians yet realise that if we are not protesting we are, as democrats, in fact consenting.

George MacLeod, founder of the Iona Community, 1962

'THANKS FOR SAYING NOTHING'

The spirituality of those who care for the dying must be the spirituality of the companion, of the friend who walks alongside, helping, sharing, and sometimes just sitting, empty-handed, when he would rather run away. It is the spirituality of presence, of being alongside, watchful, available, of being there.

Shelia Cassidy

What people need most is for others to 'hang in there' in their anguish and suffering. I am convinced that those who ask these questions know there are no answers. But they have seen people who can't handle the anxiety this creates simply leave them in their confusion. Healing takes place by staying with it while others run away.

No words, no platitudes, no biblical quotation can take the pain away. But the fact is people already know that there is nothing you can say. It is already part of our common humanity. And they have seen others turn away, embarrassed by their uselessness. Anyone who moves towards that broken person, and is not repulsed by their cries or their own sense of inadequacy – who, as I have said, is prepared to step over the threshold of the place they inhabit – gives confidence that they do have something to offer at moments of utter despair and reassurance that all is not lost.

It is not the voice which says: 'Don't just stand there, do something' which needs to be heeded. It is the voice which says: 'Don't do something, don't even say anything, just stand there, sit there, be there, in their need.' And it works.

Tom Gordon, chaplain with the Marie Curie hospice in Edinburgh, and a member of the Iona Community

Dear Joyce,

Thank you so much for coming to see me tonight. I know it wasn't easy for you, because you've had your own struggles to face recently. But you came – and so many others haven't bothered. Thanks for the hug, and the tears. I needed to cry with you, and I'm so glad you weren't stiff and awkward like some have been. And thanks for saying nothing, and allowing the silence to help. I don't need words. I've heard platitudes till I could scream. I just needed to be held by someone who understood, and to feel safe again. I wish there were more people like you, people who were human and who didn't try too hard. I really felt God was with us when you were here.

Thank you for all you've done to help me when I needed it most. I hope I can be as understanding and do the same for you some day.

With much love,
Edith

From Tom Gordon

February 21

DANCING IN THE STREETS

When my time comes
please, please, please
no penguin parades,
no solemn posturing:
but folk in jeans,
children playing, babies crying
and dancing in the streets.

Ian M Fraser, a member of the Iona Community

Love is not changed by death and nothing is lost
and all in the end is harvest.

Edith Sitwell

February 22

THE WORLD'S ICING SUGAR

The recurring tragedy of Christian history is that the Church, called by its Lord to be in the world but not of it, has, more often than not, been of the world but not in it.

The Church has seldom been absorbed by the world as salt is absorbed, giving it a new taste. It has usually been happy to be the world's icing sugar, somewhat sweetening the intolerable but changing nothing.

Paul Oestreicher

Prayer

Forgiving God, we believe that you called us
to be salt and light;
that you offer us time and space and strength
to begin again.

From an Agape service, *Iona Abbey Worship Book*

Protect me, O Lord,
my boat is so small
and your sea is so big

The Fisherman's Prayer, France

Pray to God but continue to row to the shore.

Danish proverb

JESUS MEANS FREEDOM

In the four gospels the name 'Jesus' occurs almost six hundred times and the composite name 'Jesus Christ' only four. While we think of the name 'Jesus' as very special, in Jesus's own time and society it was extremely common – it was the Greek form of three Old Testament names, Joshua, Jehoshua and Yeshua. Think of it as equivalent to the Glasgow name for everyman, 'Jimmy', or the universal 'John Smith'. It has suggestions of profound humanity, of Jesus as *everyman, the human being.*

The name Jesus also had a particular meaning among his people. It was a name of honour and significance. Joshua was the inheritor of Moses's task in leading the people of Israel into freedom and promise after their deliverance from Egypt, a task which he fulfilled. The name means 'God is my help' or 'The one who saves'. 'Jesus' means freedom.

Leith Fisher, a member of the Iona Community

February 25

PARADOX

We are omnipotent,
able to order and destroy
according to our design.

Yet the turn of the leaf in morning sun
and the catch in our throat
drives us to our knees
and into prayer.

Yvonne Morland, a member of the Iona Community

All is silent.
in the still and soundless air,
I fervently bow to my Almighty God.

Bing Xin (Hsieh Ping-hsin), 1900–1999, China

February 26

Either we walk on the poor and we'll end with Hiroshima, or we walk with the
poor which will end in Transfiguration.

Source unknown

February 27

PRAYER

O Lord,
please give me
eyes that see,
ears that hear,
a heart that cares,
and arms that open wide
and accept and forgive
even me.

Allan Gordon, a member of the Iona Community

February 28

By Christ or any other name
the truth would always be
the same

Sydney Carter

Isolation of unemployment

I punish myself most harshly when I am unemployed; of course, getting a job could be the easy way around this, but finding a job is becoming ever increasingly difficult.

I read a statistic about unemployment today and that was that 58% of adults in a certain district in these parts were unemployed. Being unemployed is a somewhat discriminated against position. First one appears as a statistic and secondly as perhaps a dubious character that really deserves the condition and all the labels that get stuck automatically onto that person … As I spend more time in the isolation of unemployment the less I hear from the people I once knew, the distances between friends who once shared interests grows, as the economic power to pursue those interests vanishes …

So the question of how one behaves towards the self while unemployed is important. People do commit suicide under such conditions, when the hatred and hopelessness appear insurmountable within the self.

David Scott, a volunteer with the Iona Community

March 1

Is not this the fast that I choose: to loose the bonds of injustice, to undo the thongs of the yoke, to let the oppressed go free, to break every yoke? Is it not to share your bread with the hungry, and to bring the homeless poor into your house; when you see the naked, to cover them, and not hide yourself from your own kin? Then your light shall break forth like the dawn, and your healing shall spring forth quickly; your vindicator shall go before you, the glory of the Lord shall be your rear guard. Then you shall call, and the Lord will answer; you shall cry for help, and he will say, Here I am.

Isaiah 58:6–9 (NRSV)

When politics and policies are biased to the poor
THEN SHALL THE LIGHT SHINE FORTH LIKE THE DAWN
When none go hungry and good food is for all
THEN SHALL THE LIGHT SHINE FORTH LIKE THE DAWN
When all have a safe place to call home and feel welcome
THEN SHALL THE LIGHT SHINE FORTH LIKE THE DAWN

Rachel McCann

March 2

These are reputedly the last words spoken by John Wesley before he died, and they are precious to the hearts of many Methodists like myself:

'And the best of all is – God is with us.'

From Richard Sharples, current warden of Iona Abbey

In work and worship
GOD IS WITH US
Gathered and scattered
GOD IS WITH US
Now and always
GOD IS WITH US. AMEN

Responses from the Iona Community's Act of Prayer

March 3

NOT COUNTING THE WOMEN AND CHILDREN

I love the story of the feeding of the multitude by the lake, not least for the bit that says, 'everyone ate, and had enough'. It is, I think, one of the most beautiful lines in the Bible, this picture of sufficiency, of sharing – 'everyone ate, and had enough'. But the story also demonstrates, simply and rather appallingly, two thousand years of a particular blindness of Christian history: 'the number who ate was about five thousand men, *not counting the women and children.'* (Or, as the Jerusalem Bible has it, 'to say nothing of the women and children' (Matt 14:21). What a history of exclusion that sums up, of people who are not counted, who have been, and continue to be, invisible in so many ways – in their poverty, in their unnoticed labour, in their wasted potential … Women all over the world have been reading the Bible and the history of the church from another angle, rediscovering hidden histories, the silenced voices, the notes on the margins. They are seeking the God of Jesus Christ, the motherly God who comes close in the Word made flesh. They are seeking the women and men whose spirituality is one of hope, of courage, of compassion, of inclusion, of persistence and resistance. They are drinking from these wells being uncovered in many places, in many traditions, in the wisdom of the body and the wisdom of the earth ...

Kathy Galloway, a member of the Iona Community

Blessing

May Sophia, God's wisdom,
guide you,
May Shekinah, God's presence,
surround you,
May Holy Ruach, God's breathing,
enable you to walk
towards the light
of the living God.

Elisabeth C. Miescher, a member of the Iona Community

March 4

BROTHER, SISTER

Brother, sister, let me serve you
    let me be as Christ to you;
pray that I may have the grace to
    let you be my servant too.

We are pilgrims on a journey,
    and companions on the road;
we are here to help each other
    walk the mile and bear the load.

I will hold the Christ-light for you
in the night-time of your fear;
I will hold my hand out to you,
speak the peace you long to hear.

I will weep when you are weeping;
when you laugh I'll laugh with you;
I will share your joy and sorrow
till we've seen this journey through.

When we sing to God in heaven
we shall find such harmony,
born of all we've known together
of Christ's love and agony.

Brother, sister, let me serve you,
let me be as Christ to you;
pray that I may have the grace to
let you be my servant too.

Richard Gillard
A song often sung in Iona Abbey.

March 5

OF THE HEART

It is not for its structures that the church is to be valued, but for the Word, its faith. The church is firstly and finally a matter not of structure but of the heart.

John Miller, former Moderator of the Church of Scotland, and minister of Castlemilk East

Can we create safe places to listen and share, not with patronising concern which leaves the structures of domination and control intact, but attentive to the possibility and hope of transforming justice? Will our churches be fortresses of refuge for the powerful perpetrators of violence, or communities of courage, where hospitality is offered, and diversity celebrated, and abuse confronted with honesty, care and integrity?

Lesley Orr, a member of the Iona Community

ALL ARE WELCOME

Let us build a house where love can dwell
and all can safely live,
a place where saints and children tell
how hearts learn to forgive.
Built of hope and dreams and visions,
rock of faith and vault of grace;
here the love of Christ shall end divisions:
 All are welcome, all are welcome,
 all are welcome in this place.

Let us build a house where prophets speak,
and words are strong and true,
where all God's children dare to seek
to dream God's reign anew.
Here the cross shall stand as witness
and as symbol of God's grace;
here as one we claim the faith of Jesus:
 All are welcome, all are welcome,
 all are welcome in this place.

Let us build a house where love is found
in water, wine and wheat:
a banquet hall on holy ground
where peace and justice meet.
Here the love of God, through Jesus,
is revealed in time and space;
as we share in Christ the feast that frees us:
All are welcome, all are welcome,
all are welcome in this place.

Let us build a house where hands will reach
beyond the wood and stone
to heal and strengthen, serve and teach,
and live the Word they've known.
Here the outcast and the stranger
bear the image of God's face;
let us bring an end to fear and danger:
All are welcome, all are welcome,
all are welcome in this place.

Let us build a house where all are named,
their songs and visions heard
and loved and treasured, taught and claimed
as words within the Word.
Built of tears and cries and laughter,
prayers of faith and songs of grace,
let this house proclaim from floor to rafter:
All are welcome, all are welcome,
all are welcome in this place.

Marty Haugen
A song often sung at the welcome service in Iona Abbey.

FAIRTRADE FORTNIGHT

Regimes depend for their power on the control of resources, both material and financial. This is where the power of the consumer can be so effective. From the sailing of medical supplies to Hanoi at the height of the Vietnam war to a small group of people who are repeatedly and courageously breaking sanctions on Iraq, there have always been people willing to defy crippling blockades. From Nestlé products to GM foods we are now well aware of the power of boycott. During the time of French nuclear tests, I was on a flight between Edinburgh and Brussels. The air hostess asked if I would like red or white wine, and when I asked if it was French she replied: 'Oh no, madam, there's been far too much protest for our airline to stock French wine.'

Helen Steven, a member of the Iona Community

Prayer

Jesus calls us
To leave the past
JESUS CALLS US TO HOPE

Jesus calls us
To travel lightly
JESUS CALLS US TO FAITH

Jesus calls us
To live fairly
JESUS CALLS US TO JUSTICE

Jesus calls us
To risky living
JESUS CALLS US TO LIFE

Ruth Burgess, a member of the Iona Community

March 7

SEEDS OF HOPE

Take time to be,
to feel,
to listen to the water, air and earth:
    creation's treasure-store.
They're wounded for the want
of being listened to;
they cry
and too few hear;
they slowly die
and too few mourn.

And yet
through those who give attention,
who stretch both hands
to touch, embrace and tend;
through those who marvel, reverence and kneel
and cup the water,
feel the breath of heaven,
and hear the humming earth,

a healing comes
and there are seeds of hope:
there is tomorrow
germinating in today.

Be still.
Be loving.
Persevere.
Be true
to your connectedness.
Be you.

Take time to be,
to feel,
to listen to the stories, dreams and thoughts
    of those who have no voice.
They're wounded for the want
of being listened to;
they cry
and too few hear;
they slowly die
and too few mourn.

And yet
through those who give attention,
who stretch both hands
to touch, embrace and tend;
through those who labour, claim their dignity
and drink the cup of suffering,
who breathe the winds of change,
and earth their dreams in struggle,

healing comes
and there are seeds of hope:
there is tomorrow
germinating in today.

Be still.
Be just –
participating
in their truth.
In finding them,
you find yourself.

Kate Compston

A THIN BLACK LINE

In Durham Cathedral a thin black line is set into the marble floor near the back of the building, far from the altar. It marked the boundary beyond which women were prohibited to venture. That control has not just been a matter of gender, and it has been imposed in the name of Jesus Christ both to exclude and to incorporate subjugated peoples in mission stations and slave planta-tions; in religious institutions where children were 'assimilated' by forcible removal from their families to be brought up as white Christians. Dispossessed or disabled, gay and lesbian, deaf and blind: so many for whom the words, symbols and dynamics of worship have been disorienting and disempowering, failing to name, address or celebrate the realities of their lives. And historically the hierarchies, rituals and structures of the church have been used to interpret and legitimise social structures of mastery – patriarchy, colonisation, capitalism – by linking them to the sacred and claiming them to be ordained by God.

Lesley Orr, a member of the Iona Community

March 9

WE ALONE

We alone can devalue gold
by not caring
if it falls or rises
in the market place.
Whenever there is gold
there is a chain, you know,
and if your chain
is gold
so much the worse
for you.

Feathers, shells
and sea-shaped stones
are all as rare.
This could be our revolution:
To love what is plentiful
as much as
what's scarce.

Alice Walker

The modernist myth of perpetual progress perished in the collapse of the twin towers.

Ron Ferguson, a member of the Iona Community

HOW SHOULD ONE LIVE?

Leader 1:   Seated around a table,
Jesus taught his friends about welcoming and being welcomed:
as companions they argued and laughed and told stories.

Leader 2:   Walking the road,
Jesus called his followers, challenged and encouraged them:
as companions they learned about God's way and God's love.

ALL: SEATED AROUND THE TABLE,
WALKING ALONG THE ROAD,
WE WILL LEARN, WE WILL LAUGH, WE WILL BE NOURISHED:
WE WILL GIVE AND RECEIVE WELCOME IN GOD'S NAME.

Responses used in Iona Abbey, by Jan Sutch Pickard, former warden of Iona Abbey

How should one live?
Live welcoming all.

Mechtild of Magdeburg, medieval Christian mystic

March 12

Justice is important, but supper is essential.

Ed Loring, The Open Door Community, Atlanta, Georgia

March 13

To refuse to struggle against the evil of the world
is to surrender your humanity.
To struggle against the evil of the world with the weapons of the evil-doer
is to enter your humanity.
To struggle against the evil of the world with the weapons of God
is to enter your divinity.

Mahatma Gandhi

Prayer

Lord, make us instruments of your peace:
where there is hatred, let us sow love;
where there is injury, pardon;
where there is discord, union;
where there is doubt, faith;
where there is despair, hope;
where there is darkness, light;
where there is sadness, joy

St Francis of Assisi

"So what do you believe in?
Nothing fixed or final,
all the while I
travel a miracle. I doubt,
and yet
I walk upon the water."

Sydney Carter

'SPECTATING'

In the forum theatre of the Brazilian August Boal there is an exercise called 'spectating'. In it, people are divided into two groups. One group is then given a scenario to act out. The other group watches the scenario unfold, without comment, till the story ends. Then the group starts acting out the scenario again. But this time, any member of the onlooking group who thinks the action should be different, who does not agree with a particular interpretation, can stop the play, can replace one of the characters and, if they choose, alter the course of the action, bring a new perspective, a fresh direction. If no one chooses to engage in this way, the scenario runs on to its original conclusion. This is a wonderfully clear way to illustrate the point that, without action, without engagement, without the investment of our time and energy, nothing changes, no matter how passionately we feel or how strong our convictions. We can love our brothers and sisters only through what we do.

Kathy Galloway

March 16

GOD IS JUSTICE

When I first began working with justice and peace groups, I described what I was doing as 'justice and peace spirituality'. Later, I realised that there is no such thing as justice and peace spirituality. There is one God, one Spirit, a God of justice, of peace, of compassion. Any spirituality which ignores issues of justice and peace cannot be of God.

Gerard Hughes

God is justice.

Julian of Norwich

March 17
St Patrick's Day

Christ be with me,
Christ within me,
Christ behind me,
Christ before me,
Christ beside me,
Christ to win me,
Christ to comfort and restore me,
Christ beneath me,
Christ above me,
Christ in quiet,

Christ in danger,
Christ in hearts of all that love me,
Christ in the mouth of friend and stranger.

St Patrick, version by Cecil Frances Alexander

Every day is a messenger from God.

Russian proverb

THE CORRYMEELA COMMUNITY

The Corrymeela Community has for years provided a safe space in Northern Ireland, neutral ground in which people who are not able to meet freely and without fear on their own territory can encounter one another, not as labels of sects but as fellow human beings in a spirit of respect, dialogue and learning. The need for such safe places is not restricted to Northern Ireland. In a dangerously divided world, they are needed everywhere. In their act of dedication, Corrymeela members commit themselves to modelling such reconciliation in their own lives:

We surrender ourselves to the Spirit of Jesus to overcome our own divisions and make us instruments of His peace.

Kathy Galloway

March 20

If we could read the secret history of our enemies, we should find in each person's life sorrow and suffering enough to disarm all hostility.

Henry Wadsworth Longfellow (1807–1882)

March 21
The first day of Spring

THANKSGIVING

For the greening of trees
and the gentling of friends
we thank you, O God.

For the brightness of field
and the warmth of sun
we thank you, O God.

For work to be done
and laughter to share,
we thank you, O God.

We thank you, and know
that through struggle and pain
in the slippery path of new birth
hope will be born
and all shall be well.

Kate McIlhagga, a member of the Iona Community

The families I was working with were as thirsty for dignity as they were for running water.

Father Joseph Wresinski (1917-1988), founder of ATD Fourth World

Let justice flow like a stream, and righteousness like a river that never goes dry.

Amos 5:24 (GNB)

'Young man, you'll be damn lucky to get into heaven without dragging your damn little Pomeranian after you.'

George MacLeod, in response to a heckler at Glasgow University Union who shouted: 'Dr MacLeod, will my dog go to heaven?'

DOORS OF HOPE

Cathedral doors, over the centuries, have provided opportunities for skilled woodworkers to interpret the great moments of salvation history in carved figures, so that the learned and unlearned might be instructed.

Yet none that I have seen can match the doors of Oscar Romero's cathedral in San Salvador.

Traditional doors may have once stood there. The hostility to Romero and what he stood for could well mean that the original doors had been disfigured by being hacked or burned. What I do know is that the doors which I saw, shortly after the Archbishop's murder, provided an image which will stick in my mind for ever.

They were made of plain planks of wood. Instruction in what pertained to the kingdom of God had been registered not with hammer and chisel, but with aerosols. Here again the learned and unlearned could understand. Every available space was covered by the cries of the people:

'End the oppression' ... 'Down with the Junta' ...
'Justice or Death' ... 'Our Hope is in God' ...
'God is the Judge not the Junta.'

Ian M Fraser, a member of the Iona Community

March 25

SHE HERALDS A REVOLUTION

The leaders of the world exult in possessing a power undreamt of in all human history ... they are convinced that peace comes from the possession of power – military, economic and political. In this they place their trust and hope.

... But the gospels tell a different story. When Mary sings her enfleshment of God in an outburst of joy, she heralds a revolution: 'My soul magnifies the Lord, and my spirit rejoices in God my Saviour ... surely from now on all generations will call me blessed ... he has shown strength with his arm; he has scattered the proud in the thoughts of their hearts. He has brought down the powerful from their thrones, and lifted up the lowly; he has filled the hungry with good things, and sent the rich away empty. (Luke 1: 46-53, NRSV)

These words are truly extraordinary. Either they mean what they say, or they are empty rhetoric. And if they mean what they say, then they are proclaiming in the incarnation a reversal of all worldly notions of status and worth, an end to all domination.

Paul spells out the same good news clearly: 'There is no longer Greek and Jew ... barbarian, Scythian, slave and free; but Christ is all and in all!' (Col 3:11, NRSV)

Brian Quail, a member of the Iona Community

March 26

Readings for Mother's Day

ENEMY OF APATHY

She sits like a bird, brooding on the waters,
Hovering on the chaos of the world's first day;
She sighs and she sings, mothering creation,
Waiting to give birth to all the Word will say.

She wings over earth, resting where she wishes,
Lighting close at hand or soaring through the skies;
She nests in the womb, welcoming each wonder,
Nourishing potential hidden to our eyes.

She dances in fire, startling her spectators,
Waking tongues of ecstasy where dumbness reigned;
She weans and inspires all whose hearts are open,
Nor can she be captured, silenced or restrained.

For she is the Spirit, one with God in essence,
Gifted by the Saviour in eternal love;
She is the key opening the scriptures,
Enemy of apathy and heavenly dove.

John L. Bell & Graham Maule

As truly as God is our Father, so truly is God our Mother.

Julian of Norwich

'All...ah, All...ah, All...ah. 'A young mother walks slowly round the room, a
baby on her hip, as she tries to quieten her crying child with the name of Allah.
As Muslim mothers must have done for centuries.

Stanley Hope, from an article

March 27

Power/money/resources
are a gift, given for a time,
to bring change –
not to preserve the way things are,
not to return to the way things were
BUT
that we may

receive
and live
and give

Statement from a Reflection Group at the Council for World Mission Assembly, Ayr, Scotland, 2003, formulated by David Coleman, a member of the Iona Community

March 28

We are not consumers of what God has made; we are in communion with it.

Go for a walk.
Get wet.
Dig the earth.

Rowan Williams, Archbishop of Canterbury

March 29

SINGING MY BLUES AWAY

If I sing out my pain, will it go away?
If I open my heart, will the sorrow stray?
When I sob my story in a musical way,
I'm singing my blues away.

Well I've talked it through till my throat is dry,
I have analysed every look and sigh,
I've examined the how and the where and the why,
Now I'm singing my blues away.

I have been advised, but the ache's still in place,
And I've tried being brave with a smile on my face,
I'm tired of feeling that empty space,
So I'm singing my blues away.

My heart's been sealed with a lock and a key,
And the only one who can release it is me,
I'm going to cut out that pain and set it free
By singing my blues away.

Kathy Galloway

March 30

'Is it possible to live calmly and happily when you know that two-thirds of human beings are suffering, hungry and poor?'

Leonardo Boff

March 31

Mar tobar glé trí chroí na lice
Brúchtann an dóchas trí chroí an dhuine.

Like a clear spring through the heart of a stone
Hope breaks out through the human heart.

Irish traditional poem, translation by Rosemary Power, a member of the Iona Community

April

April 1

We do not see things as they are, we see things as we are.

The Talmud

April 2

GOD THE FATHER, GOD THE HOLY SPIRIT ...

'Where is God?' Jules Monchanin, the founder of the Shantivanam ashram, one day asked a group of children.

The children answered him this way:
The Christian children pointed at the sky.
The Hindu children pointed to their hearts.

A story Bede Griffiths used to tell in the meditation hall at Shantivanam

April 3

For you, deep stillness of the silent island
For you, deep blue of the desert skies
For you, flame red of the rocks and stones
For you, sweet water from hidden springs

From the edges seek the heartlands
and when you're burnt by the journey
may the cool winds of the hovering Spirit
soothe and replenish you.

In the name of Christ, in the name of Christ.

Julie Perrin, Australia

April 4

Eat and drink together,
talk and laugh together,
enjoy life together,
but never call it friendship
until you have wept together.

An African saying

April 5

MIRACULOUS HEALING

For me all healing is amazing, miraculous if you like. The process by which our bodies and minds can be repaired fills me with awe. The complexity of the process of repair of even a small cut, a minor upset, seems to me so much more wonderful because it happens from within. The potential for wholeness and fullness of life is present within the individual cells of our bodies.

Dr Margaret Stewart, a member of the Iona Community

April 6

Jesus did not say: You will not be assailed, you will not be belaboured, you will not be disquieted, but he said: You will not be overcome.

Julian of Norwich

April 7
World Health Day

I saw a report from one area where nearly 500 people, including many children, had died of dysentery. Dysentery is not some incurable disease. It is a product of malnutrition, poverty, lack of adequate health care and disease. An angry community worker was suing the regional government for negligence.

Prayer will not make it go away. Nor will hand-outs. There are vast resources in India, but they are not well distributed. It is an issue of justice and political change. What does it mean to be the church of Jesus in this situation?

Ron Ferguson, a member of the Iona Community, an excerpt from his reflections on a trip to India

April 8

For the Church in any country to retreat from politics is nothing short of heresy. Christianity is political or it is not Christianity.

Desmond Tutu

PEOPLE SHOULD ARRIVE IN JERUSALEM IN TEARS

The coach grumbled up from the depths of the Rift Valley ascending 2000 feet in a few miles to the outskirts of Jerusalem. We'd taken the old road from Jericho with glimpses of the track deep in the Wadi Quilt. The track, scene of the Good Samaritan story, clung to the steep rock face.

Sinai was now far behind. After its cleansing effect it was a shock to take the Bethany road into Jerusalem. Noisy. Dirty. Ill-kept. Dogs everywhere. The city's backside.

Yet we were travelling over holy ground. We were ascending the Mount of Olives. The coach stopped. We had to walk the last mile. It is called the Trail of Tears.

And then into sight came Jerusalem. A glorious tortured city. A city with the word PEACE in its name but a place where there is no peace.

As we toiled over the summit – the ancient pilgrim prayer was heard:

'Pray for the peace of Jerusalem
... for the sake of my relatives and friends I will say

Peace be with you ...

For the sake of the House of the Lord,
I will seek your good.

(Psalm 121)

Lower down the slope we entered the Dominus Flevit church. Above the altar there is a stone relief of Jesus, grim-faced, coming into the city riding a donkey.

He is in tears.
Head bowed.

He is oblivious to the crowds.

The crowds do not see his mood.
They do not hear the tone in his voice.
They only see the arrival of a triumphant king.

He was a king who wept on his donkey.

Palm Sunday songs should have tears in them.

John Rackley, a member of the Iona Community

April 10

A PRAYER FOR THE CITY

The vision is of a city renewed.
    A city which is the 'home of God'
with all that makes a city home
    and a house a hearth.
Father for this we pray:
for a city with space
with space to live,
    with space to gather and space to withdraw,
    with space to meet and space to be alone,
    with space to dance and space to sing,
    with space to play, and space to enjoy,
    with space for you, O God.

We pray for a city
    with space for houses and space for trees,
    with space for green and space for grass,
    with space for colour and fruit and flower,
    with space to work and space to rest,
    and space for you, O God.

We pray for homes
    with father and mother,
    and children and friends,
    with health and wholeness
    and love and laughter,
    with neighbours and nearness
    with you, O God.
    Amen

Graeme Brown, a member of the Iona Community
This prayer was written when Graeme was working as a minister in the East end
of Glasgow.

April 11

ETERNAL MOMENT

It was late in spring … Once in my life I have actually seen a crop agrowing and
heard the deep rustle of its growth. And, though it was spring, some foretaste
of that lush magic was in the air. Cool and inexpressibly still: yet I felt the whole
earth burgeoning to life. And there, before me, silhouetted against a pink sky,
was a lamb without blemish on iridescent green: motionless. All the breath

went from me. I was waiting to see a flag held in its forefoot and upright across its flank: sealed for St John. It was not there, of course: the flag. It was just a lamb, upright: yet motionless as if it had been slain. All in the April evening, I thought on the Lamb of God.

I do not think I will see the Abbey when I come to cross the final bourne. But I think I will remember that eternal moment. It was nature, just nature, preaching the gospel to a man.

Prayer

Once more we give thanks,
for earth and sea and sky in harmony of colour,
the air of the eternal seeping through the physical,
the everlasting glory dipping into time.
For nature resplendent:
growing beasts, emergent crops, singing birds,
We bless Thee.

For swift running tides,
resistant waves,
Thy spirit on the waters:
O Lord: how marvellous are Thy works.
In majesty hast Thou created them.

George MacLeod, adapted

The reputation of the community on Iona grew quickly, and curious visitors and pilgrims flocked to the island. Hospitality was a sacred monastic tradition, and Adomnán reports how Columba cancelled a fast day to give hospitality to 'a certain troublesome guest'. He also recounts the saint's legendary ability to sense when a guest was about to arrive.

On a day when the tempest was fierce and the sea exceedingly boisterous, the saint gave orders, saying, 'Prepare the guest chamber quickly and draw water to wash the stranger's feet.' One of the brethren enquired, 'Who can cross the Sound safely on so perilous and stormy a day!' The saint made answer: 'The Almighty has given a calm evening in this tempest to a certain holy and excellent man who will arrive here among us before evening.' And lo! that same day the ship for which the brethren had some time been looking out arrived according to the saint's prediction and brought St Cainnech. The saint went down with his brethren to the landing place and received him with all honour and hospitality.

Hospitality was sacred, because Christ was the stranger. The Gaelic Rune of Hospitality puts it thus:

We saw a stranger yesterday,
we put food in the eating place,
drink in the drinking place,
music in the listening place,
and, with the sacred name of
the triune God,
he blessed us and our house,
our cattle and our dear ones.

Ron Ferguson

April 13

Isn't it odd? When you understand the needed ingredients for life, someone wants to put nails in your hands or bullets in your head.

Ed Loring, The Open Door Community, Atlanta, Georgia

Prayer

Lord,
keep me awake.

Ralph Morton

April 14

HOPE

You spoke of hope,
how we must identify with it –
be it for an unbelieving world.
Can you tell me how to live
that hope in Highgate*?
Can you bring that hope out of
the pulpit and explain it
so that those without money, without
jobs, without power, without
purpose can understand?
Can you tell me what hope there is
for kids whose parents are never
there when they need them,

for the old folk frightened to
walk to the shops,
for men and women whose jobs
have gone – and with them their dignity.
I read, long ago, that only a
suffering Christ makes sense.
Tonight the suffering of Highgate
is around me and in me
and a triumphant risen Christ is offensive,
for Highgate is an eternal Good Friday
and even Jesus broke down on the cross.
We are not ready for hope – not yet –
and some of us are not sure that we
will recognise it when it comes.

Ruth Burgess, a member of the Iona Community

* The Highgate in this poem is an area of Birmingham.

Lord, take my soul, but the struggle continues.

Last words of Ken Saro-Wiwa

Prayer

Christ of every suffering heart,
bless our awakening
as we begin to
discern more and more
your presence of life
within
the tortured

the abandoned
the persecuted
the imprisoned
the exploited
the betrayed
the violated
the abused
the silenced.

Peter Millar, a member of the Iona Community

April 15

NEXT YEAR IN JERUSALEM

Will there still be bombing and suicides
next year in Jerusalem?
Will your people be fighting to the death
next year in Jerusalem?
Will there be blood, like your blood, and
bodies, like yours, broken and maimed in
the streets of your city,
next year in Jerusalem?
Will women still weep in public as they grieve
for their sons, like they grieved for you,
next year in Jerusalem?
Will we be gathered together and praying
because of what happened that year
in Jerusalem?

Alison Swinfen, a member of the Iona Community

RESURRECTION THOUGHTS

The resurrection of the dead is no more miraculous than the birth of a child. Walking on water is no more miraculous than walking on earth.

Roger Gray, a member of the Iona Community

[The Resurrection is] an invitation to recognise one's victim as one's hope. The crucified is God's chosen: it is with the victim, the condemned, that God identifies, and it is in the company of the victim, so to speak, that God is to be found and nowhere else ...

Rowan Williams, Archbishop of Canterbury

Easter Sunday, 2005, Aylesbury

The question is not: Did it happen? It *happens* every time we tell the Jesus story and when we share our own stories. It's in the remembering, the letting go and the moving on. It happens every time the green bursts out of the winter dark, buds open and daffodils yellow the earth. It happens in the excitement of ordinary meetings and the conversations of home. It happens every time someone forgives, and heals another, every time bread is shared. It happens every time I'm surprised by a rainbow, feel new life in the air or that unexplainable warming in my heart. It happens when I light a candle and let go my dreams into the dark spaces. The flame stays when I have gone, connecting me with others, kindling hope in their hearts. It burns itself out but does not die.

I know resurrection happens. The question might be: What is it? I don't know what resurrection is, and I don't need to know. I believe it is something like coming through on the far side of a day; that it comes quietly in moments of light where love is strong to bear regrets and banish fears.

Hope is resurrection in waiting.

Joy Mead, a member of the Iona Community

April 17

Remembering his death
How we choose to live
Will decide its meaning

WH Auden

April 18

CHURCH FOR THE WORLD

The Christian Church which follows Christ's mission to the world is engaged also in following Christ's service of the world. It has its nature as the body of the crucified and risen Christ only where in specific acts of service it is obedient to its mission to the world. Its existence is completely bound to the fulfilling of its service. For this reason it is nothing in itself, but all that it is, it is in existing for others. It is the Church of God where it is a Church for the world.

Jürgen Moltmann

Prayer

Lord God,
whose Son was content to die
to bring new life,
have mercy on your church,
which will do anything you ask,
anything at all,
except die to be reborn.

Lord Christ,
forbid us unity
which leaves us where we are
and as we are:
welded into one company
but extracted from the battle;
engaged to be yours,
but not found at your side.

Holy Spirit of God,
reach deeper than our inertia and fears:
release us into the freedom of the children of God.
Amen

Ian M Fraser, a member of the Iona Community

April 19

WHERE ARE YOUR WOUNDS?

– I don't worry about the wounds. When I go up there, which is my intention, the Big Judge will say to me, Where are your wounds? and if I say I haven't any, he will say, Was there nothing to fight for? I couldn't face that question.

Alan Paton

April 20

WHAT DEATH AND RESURRECTION MEAN
From a basic Christian community in Panama

'We find people taking on themselves a ministry based on what has been their own personal experience of resurrection in a particular area of life. For instance, Fidel Gonzales is extremely adept at talking to people who are sick and dying, who need someone to put an element of hope in their lives. Fidel is good because he himself has twice been close to death. A car turned over and he was almost killed. His brain was badly damaged; one side was knocked out, and the doctors thought he wouldn't be able to speak. However, he is left-handed, and as there is some kind of relationship between the right side of the brain and the left side of the body, so he came out of it. It was an experience of resurrection for him. Slowly he learned to walk again, to write again. To hear him talk about his own experience, or talk to a person about what sickness implies, what death and resurrection mean, is a fantastic experience because *it is something he has lived*. He can fulfil ministry in this particular way.

'Favio and Adelina are a couple who have lived out the difficulties of marriage. This is a second marriage for Adelina. The first was an absolute disaster. To find in a marriage relationship what she has found with Favio! Then to see what Favio has become! Here is a man who stutters badly, all of a sudden there he is, standing up and performing a liturgy of the word, giving communion to an area group! This all comes out of the reality of resurrection in marriage, resurrection in a portion of life which they have lived out together. Hear Favio talk to a young couple who are going to be married – this man who couldn't speak before: 'Now look, marriage is a completely different experience, nobody can tell you what it is going to be like. It is going to be yours. You must put the elements of creativity in it.' To listen to him speak to those about to be married is something to live for! ...'

From Ian M Fraser

'I was brought up to see ministers as awesome – to respect the cloth. But I know now everybody has a ministry. It's up to you what you make of it.'

Attie McKecknie, an early member of the Iona Community

April 21

In every person it is possible to see Christ's own face. Nothing has more beauty than a face that a whole life of struggle has rendered transparent.

Brother Roger, Taizé Community

HOW WILL THE MOUNTAINS JUDGE US?

To be a creature, one among many, is to come face to face with our limitations. We are not God, and God is not just an idealised version of us. God is other, and speaks to us in other voices. Our judgement of the world, sometimes expressed as if we had a monopoly on divine truth, is, in truth, that which holds us most to account. In Micah 6, the prophet calls the people as if to a court of law to listen to what God is saying, and this is what God the plantiff says: 'Rise, plead your case before the mountains, and let the hills hear your voice. Hear, you mountains, the controversy of the Lord, and you enduring foundations of the earth; for the Lord has a controversy with his people, and he will contend with Israel.' There can be no clearer indication anywhere in scripture that to be creature in covenant is to be required to be in right relationship not only with our own human kind, but with the whole creation. Justice is also ecojustice. And how, then, will the mountains judge us? Will the enduring foundations of the earth find in our favour?

And we are discovering the earth is making its own judgements ... It may be no exaggeration to say that we are at a kairos, a defining moment in human history. In the midst of a hugely accelerated pace of change, we are confronting in equal measure unparalleled opportunities and unparalleled threats. Significant parts of the human population, particularly in the West, are healthier, wealthier and enjoy greater opportunities for self-realisation than ever before. At the same time, the gap between rich and poor is growing, huge parts of humanity live on the margins of destitution, uprooted peoples number tens of millions and wars and pandemics devastate dozens of countries. Social and political institutions everywhere are changing and once powerful ideologies have lost their hold. The fabric and future of life itself is facing commodification and, on one hand, the wealth of consumer nations and, on the other, the poverty of energy and resource-poor countries, have caused an ecological holocaust which threatens the continuation of the planet. In the last 25 years alone, the human species has destroyed one third of its non-renewable resources. Our actions have consequences: the destruction of rainforests leads to global warming; the pollution of lakes destroys localised eco-systems; ... floods drown and bring diseases in their wake. How will the mountains judge us? I think we are beginning to hear the answer.

Kathy Galloway, leader of the Iona Community, from a talk

Enjoy the earth gently,
enjoy the earth gently,
for if the earth is spoiled
it cannot be repaired.
Enjoy the earth gently.

Yoruba poem, West Africa

April 23

The reign of the free market is akin to the freedom of the fox in the hen-house.

Susan George

April 24

May you always notice
the dazzling, white flowers
growing up between the cracks.
And may your life be full
of little resurrections.

Neil Paynter

April 25

Christian hope is a resistance movement against fatalism.

World Council of Churches Commission on Faith and Order, Bangalore, India 1978

April 26

AMAZING GRACE

People do not have to do anything. It is all grace. It is not that there is a door which Christ has unbolted, and we, standing outside it, have to stretch out our hand, lift the latch and walk through. We are already inside.

John Austin Baker

Jesus said: My grace is sufficient for you.

Corinthians 12:9

OUTWITTED

They drew a circle to keep me out;
heretic rebel, a thing to flout.
But love and I had the wit to win.
We drew a circle that took them in.

Edwin Markham

Listening looks easy, but it's not simple. Every head is a world.

Cuban proverb

HANDFULS OF AIR

When the conquistadors settled in Guatemala they staked out the 'unclaimed land', powerful leaders dividing it between themselves. The Indians stood amazed at such foolishness. Anyone with a sense must surely realise that land is not there to be owned but to be related to. It is for all to use in due proportion, animal and human being alike. They made a joke of it at first. With their hands they shaped imaginary bundles of air and faced up to one another, saying, 'This is my portion of air, not yours. Don't try to get your hands on it.' Then they fell about laughing at the foolishness of the foreigners.

Ian M Fraser, from his travel notes

A NEW FUTURE

It can well be argued that globalisation and the domination of the super-powers, or consumerism and materialism, are our modern equivalents of occupation by the Roman Empire.

Leith Fisher

The task of prophetic ministry is to nurture, nourish, and evoke a consciousness and perception alternative to the consciousness and perception of the dominant culture around us ... the formation of an alternative community with an alternative consciousness is so that the dominant community may be criticised and ultimately dismantled ... Jesus ... practised the energising of the new future given by God. This energising was fully wrought in his resurrection, in which he embodied a new future given by God.

Walter Brueggemann

May

A person plays the share markets on the internet or in an office. In one day he might clear £1000 – or £10,000 or £100,000. He might also lose, in which case he might commit suicide or even murder. In effect he has been gambling.

Another person spends her life in a hospital, looking after accident casualties, people with hip replacements, incontinent elderly people, others with dementia, dying children. She takes home £1,400 a month.

A third person has just been recruited to the executive board of a major parastatal organisation and is paid £500,000 a year, plus bonuses based on the share price of the soon-to-be-privatised company. As they take their seats, the Chairman announces it has been decided to raise their remuneration to £700,000 to bring it into line with equivalent pay for large private companies. The new recruit makes a hash of the job, and is paid to leave with £1.5 million.

A woman tills the soil with a hoe. It is slow work in the heat. She carries a baby on her back. She is growing food for her family. She is paid nothing.

Which of these people adds the most value?

Margaret Legum, economist and member of the Iona Community

Prayer

O Christ, the master carpenter,
who at the last, through wood and nails,
purchased our whole salvation,
wield well your tools in the workshop of your world,

so that we who come rough-hewn to your bench
may here be fashioned to a truer beauty of your hand.
We ask it for your own name's sake.
Amen

Prayer from the Iona Community

May 2

REVOLUTION

One of the most exciting aspects of non-violence is that it calls forth all our creativity and imagination, all our reserves of individuality, uniqueness, courage and humour. I don't believe we have even begun to imagine the extent of the upside down world we are called to live in. We have become so familiar with the Gospel stories that we forget how utterly shocking, radical and different Jesus's lifestyle was …

Anyone involved in non-violence is engaged in changing the unjust structures of society, and surely that is revolution. As Christians we are living the Kingdom now; we are already turning the world upside down.

Helen Steven, a member of the Iona Community

Leader: Christ has come to turn the world upside down:
ALL: TO HUMBLE THE POWERFUL AND TO LIFT UP THE LOWLY.
Leader: Christ has come to turn the tables:
ALL: TO TOPPLE VAIN IDOLS AND TO STAND WITH THE POOR.
Leader: Christ has come to proclaim God's kingdom:
Men: **to feed the hungry,**
Women: **to give sight to the blind,**

Men:	**to strengthen the weary,**
Women:	**to set the prisoners free.**
Leader:	Christ has come to turn the world upside down:
ALL:	TO OVERTHROW THE PRESENT ORDER
	WITH A REVOLUTION OF LOVE.

From *Iona Abbey Worship Book*

May 3

HOPE GROWING

Hope growing,
silently, secretly,
like a child in the womb, fluttering;
putting out soft fingers,
hope, stretching, stirring.

Hope growing,
silently, secretly,
daring to breathe again
as footsteps recede
and danger retreats,
hope, stretching, stirring.

Hope growing,
silently, secretly
swelling, burgeoning, bursting
until the flower opens

the child is crowned,
the prisoner released
and hope is born.

God of all hopefulness,
for seeds of silent growth
and secret expectation,
we thank you.
Bring hope to birth in us;
release us that we may worship
in freedom and joy.

Kate McIlhagga, a member of the Iona Community

May 4

TRANSFIGURED BY CEREMONY

It is ceremony that makes life bearable for us the terror and ecstasies that lie deep in the earth, and in our earth-nourished human nature. Only the saints can encounter those 'realities'. What saves us is ceremony. By means of ceremony, we keep our foothold in the estate of man, and remain good citizens of the kingdom of the ear of corn. Ceremony makes everything bearable and beautiful for us. Transfigured by ceremony, the truths we could not otherwise endure come to us. We invite them to enter. We set them down at our tables. These angels bring gifts for the house of the soul …

George MacKay Brown

May 5

God of all mercy, you bury our past in the heart of Christ and of our future
you are going to take care.

Brother Roger, Taizé Community

Prayer

Lord, let us not dwell in the past,
nor worry about the future.
We cannot undo what is done,
we cannot foresee what will come.
Let us instead dwell in your peace,
love and be loved,
heal and be healed.
We give the past to you and rest in your forgiveness.
We give the future to you and rest in your love.
We live in your light, open our eyes that we may see.
We live in your love, let your love flow through us,
to the fulfilment of your kingdom.
Amen

Richard Moriarty, a member of the Iona Community

May 6

Love has no other desire but to fulfil itself.
But if you love and must needs have desires,

let these be your desires:
To melt and be like a running brook
that sings its melody to the night.
To know the pain of too much tenderness.
To be wounded by your own understanding of love;
and to bleed willingly and joyfully.

Kahil Gibran

May 7

INEQUALITIES MUST BE WIPED OUT

The Christian and Jewish scriptures would be virtually non-existent if we were to cut all references to the imperative to income equality and distribution. From the prophets – notably Isaiah, Jeremiah and Micah – to the teachings of Jesus of Nazareth, the constant refrain is the requirement for human beings to treat one another as though each represents the deity on earth. 'In as much as you did it to the least of these my brethren you did it unto me' implies that poverty in the midst of plenty is a sin against God. The concept of jubilee, the regular periodic forgiveness of debt, is an explicit recognition that from time to time inequalities must be wiped out and a new start made. The prophet Mohammed gave the same message.

Margaret Legum

Our economic structures do not serve the interests of the poor and that is sin, probably *the* sin of our day.

Erik Cramb, a member of the Iona Community and former chairperson of Church Action on Poverty

May 8

JUBILEE

The teaching of Jesus is that, with him, every year is Jubilee. For me, this belief was given flesh in Community Week one year when the whole congregation in Iona Abbey said these words from Luke's gospel as an affirmation of faith. Suddenly, what had been a real belief about Jesus Christ was given a new reality as a shockingly personal and specific call to discipleship:

Affirmation

The Spirit of the Lord is upon me
HE HAS CHOSEN ME TO BRING GOOD NEWS TO THE POOR.
HE HAS SENT ME TO PROCLAIM LIBERTY TO THE CAPTIVES
AND RECOVERY OF SIGHT TO THE BLIND;
TO FREE THE OPPRESSED
AND ANNOUNCE THAT THE TIME HAS COME
WHEN THE LORD WILL SAVE HIS PEOPLE
This is the word of the Lord
THANKS BE TO GOD

Kathy Galloway

May 9

If you want peace you must declare war on revenge.

Ernest Levy, survivor of Auschwitz and Belsen living in East Renfrewshire, Scotland

The Bible says that what gives value to you and me is that we are created in the image of God. That is what is intrinsic to who you are and nothing can take that away from you. You are created in the image of God. You are a God carrier. You are God's representative round here.

Desmond Tutu

Our deepest fear is not that we are inadequate.
Our deepest fear is that we are powerful beyond measure.
It is our light, not our darkness, that most frightens us.

We ask ourselves,
'Who am I to be brilliant, gorgeous, talented, fabulous?'
Actually, who are you *not* to be?
You are a child of God.

Your playing small does not serve the world.
There's nothing enlightened about shrinking
so that other people won't feel insecure around you.
We are all meant to shine, as children do.

We were born to make manifest the glory of God that is within us.
It's not just in some of us; it is in everyone!
And as we let our own light shine,
we unconsciously give other people permission to do the same.
As we are liberated from our own fear,
our presence automatically liberates others.

Marianne Williamson

May 11

Though the cause of evil prosper, yet the truth alone is strong;
Though her portion be the scaffold, and upon the throne be wrong;
Yet that scaffold sways the future, and behind the dim unknown,
Standeth God within the shadow, keeping watch above His own.

James Russell Lowell, 1845, from the hymn *Once to Every Man and Nation*, written as a protest against America's war with Mexico.

A favourite hymn of Roger Gray, a peace activist and member of the Iona Community, who died in 1986.

May 12

FORGIVENESS

Forgiveness, when it happens, is able to remove that dead weight from our past and give us back our lives. The real beauty and power of forgiveness is that it can deliver the future to us.

Richard Holloway

Without forgiveness there is no future.

Desmond Tutu

ENLIGHTENMENT

Enjoy whatever you are doing and you do it deeply ... enlightenment is not separate from washing dishes or growing lettuce. To learn to live each moment of our daily life in deep mindfulness and concentration is the practice ... we should make good use of every moment in our daily life in order to allow this insight and compassion to bloom.

Thich Nhat Hanh

Personally consumed of the here and now,
we must recover the sense of God as
Here and Now.

George MacLeod

Those of steadfast mind you keep in peace –
in peace because they trust in you.

Isaiah 26:3 (NRSV)

PRAYER

O God, you promise a world
where those who now weep shall laugh;
those who are hungry shall feast;
those who are poor now, and excluded,

shall have your kingdom for their own.
I want this world too.
I renounce despair.
I will act for change.
I choose to be included
in your great feast of life.

From Christian Aid

May 15
International Conscientious Objectors' Day

Without taxes, of course, governments would be financially crippled. In Scotland over 50% of the people refused to pay the Poll Tax, which so many considered an unjust burden on the poor, and thus played a direct part in bringing down the Conservative government. I am puzzled to know why more people who are conscientious objectors don't question Inland Revenue about the payment of the 12% of their taxes that is spent on defence.

Helen Steven, a member of the Iona Community

Why are the prisons not full of Christians breaching the peace?

Roger Gray

If we idolise wealth, then we create poverty; if we idolise success, then we create the inadequate; if we idolise power, we create powerlessness.

Thomas Cullinan, Benedictine monk and activist

ICONS

There was a gut-wrenching picture in our papers this week: a close-up of the face of an asylum-seeker who has sewn together his eyelids and his lips so he cannot see or speak or eat and drink, in protest not just at his own treatment but at the treatment of others. That really challenges my 'connectedness'. I thought at first it was a religious picture I was looking at – he looked positively Christ-like. And of course that is precisely what he is. And it touched me profoundly. And when I realised it wasn't Christ but this asylum-seeker I found myself uttering the usual crap! But I cannot let it go, and it is my icon this week! And will sit alongside the photo I cut from *The Guardian* during the Kosovo conflict of the legs (in joggers and trainers) of a young woman who climbed a hill behind her refugee camp to hang herself because she had been raped and saw no future for herself. I wanted to nail that photo on to every altar.

Helen Cook, in a letter to Peter Millar

May 18

The three phrases I should let go from my mind if I want to be serene are 'What if?', 'If only …' and 'Why me?'

Anon

May 19

What we are asked to do at present is not so much to speak of Christ as to let him live in us so that people may find him by feeling how he lives in us.

Thomas Merton

May 20

How do we measure the Church?
A fellowship in which you would be happy to die.
A fellowship in which the young find life.
A fellowship in which those who are in their prime are challenged
    and stretched.
A fellowship of love, overflowing in service.

Fergus Macpherson, from a sermon

The priority for the Church today is not liturgics …
The priority for the Church today is not structure …
The top priority for many [in the Church] is to decide where they really stand.

George MacLeod, 1989

The works which are counted good before God … to save the lives of the innocent, to repress tyranny, to defend the oppressed.

The Scots Confession, 1560

Nuclear weapons are contrary to the will of God.

General Assembly of the Church of Scotland, 2000

AT LEAST TWO SPECIES

Humankind depends upon biodiversity for food, medicines, shelter, clothing fibres and industrial products such as rubber, starches and oils, yet at present we are still prepared to allow the extinction of species in such places as Madagascar, Hawaii and Atlantic coastal Brazil. Even at home in Britain extinction is happening to plants and animals. At the Royal Botanic Gardens, Kew we have seeds in our seed bank of at least two species of plants which have become extinct in the wild since we began collecting seeds twenty-three years ago. The interrupted brome grass (*Bromus interruptus*) and the triangular club-rush (*Scirpus triqueter*) would be completely extinct if we had not collected the seeds before their demise in the wild … The actions of the next forty years regarding biodiversity will determine whether or not human life will survive on earth. If we continue at the present extinction rate of between 4,000 and 6,000 species a year, by 2030 there will be between 160,000 and 250,000 less species to hold our biosphere together or for us to use or even just enjoy.

Ghillean Prance, Science Director of the Eden Project (Cornwall), and former Director of Royal Botantic Gardens, Kew

May 23

Britain is marred by a lack of democracy, by the oppression of poor people. So what? My objections spring from my Christian socialism. I believe God created all people of equal value: it follows that all people should be given the opportunity to contribute to the shape of our society … I believe God made all people of equal worth: it follows that the resources of the Earth should be distributed as equally as possible. I am sure that God, in the person of Christ, displayed a particular concern for the poor.

Bob Holman

God stands at every time unconditionally and passionately on this side and this side only: always against the lofty and on behalf of the lowly; against those who already enjoy right and privilege and on behalf of those who are denied it and deprived of it.

Karl Barth

Stand, O stand firm
Stand, O stand firm
Stand, O stand firm
and see what the Lord can do.

Song from the Cameroons

ANYTHING ELSE WE CAN LABEL OR CONTAIN

We are sitting on a hillside at Kodai, at an open-air communion table, part of an ashram, looking out on a breathtaking view of the mountains and plains. The vista is enormous, stretching for miles and miles. It is hard to describe the sense of eternity. The vastness of the terrain and the sense of India's history make us feel very small – and yet one with it all. A bird swoops effortlessly, gracefully and slowly, like a soul released. The silence is tangible. Death itself seems almost natural, a moving into that deeper oneness. It is impossible to sit here, sensing the communion, and not feel in some way changed.

It strikes me there and then that Protestantism has too narrow a base, at least the Protestantism I have known.

It strikes me then and there that my life has too parochial a base …

It is 5:30 am. The Indian dawn is breaking. The birds are starting to sing. We are seated with the Buddhist meditators on the banks of the sacred river Cavery, listening to Hindu music.

It is indescribable. All I can say for sure is that there is no possibility of confusing the experience with a kirk service in Edinburgh.

God is disclosed in a new way. Whatever 'God' refers to, She is not Presbyterian or Christian or Buddhist or Hindu. Or anything else we can label or contain.

Ron Ferguson, extracts from *Grace and Dysentery*

I remember fifteen years ago, when Mandela was still in prison, and the news of South Africa grew grimmer by the day, as a fortress mentality developed there, and as people here felt impotent to do anything and maybe did not care too much anyway.

I remember here in this Abbey, on the last evening of the week when people gathered to celebrate communion round a table, two young men joined hands high in the air and sang *Nkosi Sikelel' iAfrika* ... God bless Africa. One was white and British – representing the nation which in South Africa introduced concentration camps to the world – and the other was black and a Xhosa whose schooling had been disrupted by township violence and whose presence in Scotland was monitored by the South African police.

And suddenly, in that action – of joining hands and singing – there was a glimpse of a new heaven and a new earth, a possibility that things could change and all would be different and that our deep prayers and our demonstrations would not be in vain. God raised up that sign.

John Bell, a member of the Iona Community

Prayer for Africa

God bless Africa:
Guard her children,
Guide her rulers,
And give her peace.
For Jesus Christ's sake.

Bishop Huddleston

QUESTION/ANSWER

Question: 'What brings beauty into your life?'

Answer: 'The Grace of God and the dreams of people who still believe they can make a difference.'

Mo Mansill, National Youth Coordinator of Presbyterian Church of Aotearoa New Zealand and a former volunteer with the Iona Community, in an interview

… when Christians find the world in a state not in accord with what it should be, their responsibility is not that it should be explained but that it should be ended.

J H Oldham

THE NEW ECONOMICS

'I am because you are'

Economics – the way that people relate to each other with regard to resources – matters a great deal. It profoundly affects what kind of society we have, and therefore how people behave and develop. That is its real importance. The pretence that this is a technical matter that can be dealt with only by 'experts' ignores the fact that we are all affected by our culture, and our culture is much influenced by the prevalent economic system.

In some respects this is similar to the way theologies are sidelined as though our spiritual lives can be separated from the rest of our existence. Reference to the teachings of the Prophet Mohammed, Jesus Christ, the Buddha or the prophets from Joshua to Malachi is sanitised into pious moments neatly fenced off from the rest of life. The African philosophy of Ubuntu is a spiritual understanding of the whole of life: 'I am because you are.' Interpretations of deeper meaning may be heard with sentimental smiling eyes and then patronised with lip service only. And yet our belief systems, including those that are implicit only, profoundly affect our behaviour and indeed our real lives. New Economics, unlike Old Economics, may be described as economics for real life.

Margaret Legum, a member of the Iona Community

May 29

And hope? Yes, our hope should be based on our memory. But we need a broader base and a steady and positive driving force. Here I see our Christian memory as a leading example: Our hope in Christ should never be based only on his miracles, his healing ministry, his feeding of crowds, his affection and his resurrection, but it should also reflect on his suffering and cross – then we shall not forget too easily the power of evil and shall be able to realise that we can hold on to our Christian hope in spite of all our very sad and excruciating evidence …

Tomas Bisek, an associate member of the Iona Community, at the World Student Christian Federation (WSCF) Centenary Conference in Edinburgh, 1995

The very poor tell us over and over again that a person's greatest misfortune is not to be hungry or unable to read, nor even to be without work. The greatest misfortune of all is to know that you count for nothing.

Joseph Wresinski (1917-1988), founder of ATD Fourth World

FORMULA FOR CHANGE

Change = Discontent+Vision+First steps+Energy (which is greater than the cost)

Source unknown

June 1

ROOTS AND WINGS

I have learnt in my own work that the first step to maturity is to be able to forgive our parents for the unwitting hurts they gave us; the next is to forgive ourselves for the unwitting hurts we gave our children – only then can we help them break the pattern.

Kay Carmichael

There are two lasting bequests we can give our children: roots and wings.

Hodding Carter, Jr (1907–1972)

June 2

FRIENDS

When I can no longer bear my loneliness, I take it to my friends.

Mechtild of Magdeburg, medieval Christian mystic

Prayer

We give thanks for our friends.
Our dear friends.
We anger each other.
We fail each other.
We share this sad earth, this tender life,
this precious time.

Such richness. Such wildness.
Together we are dragged along.
All this delight.
All this suffering.
All this forgiving life.
We hold it together.

Michael Leunig

GOD IS ...

God is love,
God is peace,
God is joy,
God is hope,
God is singing,
God is community,
God is dancing,
God is healing,
God is listening,
God is justice,
God is sunlight,
God is starlight,
God is silence,
God is laughter ...

Adapted from a song from Uganda, taught by volunteers from Uganda, in the old coffeehouse on Iona

Then afterward
I will pour out my spirit on all flesh;
your sons and your daughters shall prophesy,
your old men shall dream dreams,
and your young men shall see visions.

Joel 2:28 (NRSV)

Lord Jesus, it is so wonderful to know of the Spirit which you sent
and which even now invades our hearts.
By whose invading even now we know
that our thinking, feeling and willing
are made new.

George MacLeod

The agents of the Holy Spirit have no right to be anything but catalysts and disturbers, who help the powerful to see their weakness and the powerless to understand their strength.

Attributed to Ian M Fraser, a member of the Iona Community

Some day, after mastering the winds, the waves, the tides and gravity,
we shall harness for God the energies of love,
then for a second time in the history of the world,
we will have discovered fire.

Teilhard de Chardin

We cannot live in a world denuded of transcendence.

Peter Millar, a member of the Iona Community

HEALING SERVICE, IONA ABBEY

Although the month is June there is no great warmth
in here. Even our numbers don't help, and we are
about a hundred. The thick grey slate of the floor is chill.
The stone walls will not give way. There is a cool breeze
from the door that puckers the skin of my hands.
Now the minister lifts her arms and calls us into Community.

I have chosen to be part of this, dipping my head in prayer.
Forcibly drawing my faith away from its natural home

into the supernatural. How far can I commit?
Cancer, anorexia, infertility, she names these things.
None of us has yet accepted the unacceptable.
One by one we go forward for the laying on of hands.

The unbearable has forced its way through our bliss.
This life is all we can be sure of. We want to go on.
Heaven and hell are where we have always lived.
There has been much talk of miracles in this place.
Much talk of a thin veil between this world and the next.
We have a great sense of togetherness, of something shared.

Rain sweeps against the windows. Candle flames shiver
in the breeze but don't go out. Human sympathy exists.
In the course of a life we all rise from the dead many times.
I know I am not who I was, who I was, who I was.
No one walks on water. Everyone walks through fire.
Once again my time has arrived. I go forward and kneel.

Robert Davidson

June 8

'I feel I am a second-class citizen.'

A Muslim man in Britain, 2005

SEPARATED FOR GOD IN THE WORLD

This emphasis on withdrawal formed a strong part of the Celtic tradition. Columba would retreat to Hinba (an island still not clearly identified) as Jesus would retire to a mountain or desert. But prayer and reflection were balanced by involvement in the world's affairs. Columba, whose lineage might have allowed him to become High King of Ireland, acted as powerbroker between warring dynasties and tribes. Holiness for him was not in being separated from the world but in being separated for God in the world, a commitment which called both for involvement and reflection, as it does today.

Ian M Fraser, a member of the Iona Community

HOLY WORLDLY PEOPLE

Dietrich Bonhoeffer talks about the need for 'holy worldly' people – followers of Jesus who live in the world but who are also sustained by an arcane, or secret, discipline of prayer. 'Contemplation' or 'action' are false alternatives. Both are involved in the Christian lifestyle. A person who prays deeply will be driven to act against injustice. Similarly, a Christian who is engaged in the problems of the world will be driven to prayer. Contemplation need not be escapism, a turning one's back on the world which God loves. Prayer is at the heart of a genuine Christian radicalism – one which truly gets to the root of the matter.

Ron Ferguson

GOD'S PEACE
(From a sermon in Iona Abbey)

So often Iona is perceived as a place of peace and tranquillity. And of course, despite the frequent crowds of visitors between the jetty and the Abbey, many of us do discover this kind of peace here. I had a strong sense of it the other day walking back home towards the machair on a clear still night; in the half-darkness I could just see a tiny frog jumping across the path to keep out of my way; the croak of the corncrake penetrated the silence. And the next morning it was dry, calm and warm for the first time in a week as I went for my daily jog across the machair to Port Ban. It was so peaceful until I encroached on the territory of the oyster-catchers at the far end of the Bay at the Back of the Ocean: they shrieked at me angrily, perhaps protecting a nest, and I thought for a moment they were going to dive-bomb me rather like terns do. In one sense it was anything but peaceful; in another sense there was harmony, mutual respect, a balance of right relationships. Real peace, deep peace does have a disturbing cutting edge; it is not just a frothy, feel-good, be-nice-to-everybody business. When in our Iona service, we say, 'We will seek peace and pursue it,' we also say, 'We will not offer to God offerings that cost us nothing.' The peace that many people find here turns out to be very different from what they expected – not the rather sanitised 'God is in his heaven, all's right with the world' variety; more challenging and engaged than that. Along with the conviction that 'all shall be well, and all manner of thing shall be well' there is a surprising restlessness, a desire to move and change, the realisation that in our pursuit of God's peace it is our vocation to play a part in the process of resistance to all in today's culture and society that obstructs the fulfilment of God's purpose and the coming of the Kingdom.

Norman Shanks, former leader of the Iona Community

People come to Iona looking for peace and quiet, and go away seeking peace and justice.

A volunteer with the Iona Community

Blessing

Deep peace of the running wave to you,
deep peace of the flowing air to you,
deep peace of the quiet earth to you,
deep peace of the shining stars to you,
deep peace of the Son of Peace to you.

A Celtic blessing

Stop the Arms Trade Week

The arms race and the war industry is not divided East/West, not even North/South … It is in fact an assault on the poor.

Helen Steven

UNIVERSAL PRAYER FOR PEACE

O God,
lead us from death to life, from falsehood to truth.
Lead us from despair to hope, from fear to trust.
Lead us from hate to love, from war to peace.
Let peace fill our hearts, our world, our universe.
Amen

Based on an invocation in Sanskrit

June 12
Refugee Week

I came here with nothing and no money and I am blessed for God has provided.

An asylum-seeker from Rwanda, on receiving household goods

June 13

SPEAKING OUT

When a silence is broken in the interest of confronting injustices, what we are hearing is *prophecy*. Prophetic voices are those which read the signs of the times in the light of the justice and love of God, and speak out against all which distorts or diminishes the image of God in human beings. In doing so, they may come into conflict with the status quo, with powerful interests who have an investment in the way things are ...

Kathy Galloway, in a talk about violence against women

The violence is IN the silence, and people must summon up the courage to speak out.

Spoken by a woman who had suffered abuse

June 14

Jesus was not crucified in a cathedral between two candles, but on a cross between two thieves ...

George MacLeod

give us the grace
of gulls

soaring
over earthbound lives

when caged by fear
release us

when sick or tired
restore

when headstrong, we fight against the wind
and crash

give us grace
to fly once more

despite voices
warning us

'stay grounded
forget the sky'.

Mary Palmer

June 16

NOT FASHIONABLE

It is not particularly fashionable to speak of mutual accountability, but the Bible constantly draws us back to this truth.

Peter Millar

June 17

PRAYER

O merciful Redeemer, friend and brother,
may we know thee more clearly,
love thee more dearly,
follow thee more nearly,
for ever and ever.

Prayer of St Richard of Chichester (1197–1253)

June 18

THE TROUBLE WITH THE CHURCH

The Gospel is the answer – the Church is the problem.

Attributed to Henry Sloane Coffin (1877–1954)

The trouble with the Church today is that nobody wants to persecute it. Nobody wants to persecute it because there is nothing really to persecute it about, don't you think?

George MacLeod

Prayer

Take us outside, O Christ, outside holiness,
out to where soldiers curse and nations clash
at the crossroads of the world.
So shall this building be justified.
We ask it for your own name's sake.
Amen

George MacLeod

June 19

Pray on our knees as if only God could change the world, and then get up off our knees and live as if only we can change it.

George MacLeod

'IT DOESN'T HAPPEN TO THEM'

For genuine asylum-seekers it seems likely to become more difficult to enter the UK to seek protection. Desperate people will continue to be forced into taking enormous risks.

We are all prisoners of government xenophobia and racism. A great responsibility rests on the whole majority. Their awakening is essential.

And, although it strikes at the heart of the gospel, the churches have never risen to the challenge of the racism of the state.

I once talked with a black woman about the problems in the law. Finally, she said, 'White people aren't interested.'

I asked why.

Without hesitation she replied, 'It doesn't happen to them.'

Prayer

For our treatment of asylum-seekers,
for all who have been ignored,
humiliated, degraded by the system;
for the loss of our humanity,
we express our shame and ask forgiveness.

We commit ourselves to work for a fair
and just immigration policy

Stanley Hope, a member of the Iona Community

A STORY OF HOPE
(from Camas, the Iona Community's Adventure Centre
on the Isle of Mull, Scotland)

On a dull day in June six young men and five volunteers (full of bacon rolls) set out from 'The Ark' in Edinburgh in a mini-bus for a journey to Camas.

The Ark is a breakfast café and resource centre for homeless and ex-homeless people. We were able to accomplish this trip thanks to the generosity of many folk who had donated money, equipment and several other kindnesses.

Apart from one who was disruptive (and who left on Tuesday) the lads took to Camas like ducks to water! All the chores were done without complaint, even cleaning the loos. They missed their bacon rolls for breakfast, didn't appreciate some of the vegetarian dishes, but didn't know Laura's cottage pie was veggie. They loved the grilled veggie-burgers and the special hot chocolate.

Willie's aim was to get rid of the skunks (minks). Jimmie discovered that a cairn can show the way, as well as be a memorial to someone – so he built cairns on every walk he took. There is still one on the island opposite the kitchen and maybe several on the way to the quarry.

The kayaking was a great success. The group built a raft from old drums and looked as if they were going to set off for America! Perhaps the abseiling was enjoyed most. They have treasured photos of each one descending the cliff. They didn't want to walk much – they do more than enough of that around Edinburgh. They liked fishing and just sitting with the staff and volunteers, chatting and drinking tea. Jimmie made some wonderful rolls for the last evening meal, with some help and laughter from Laura.

For us it was a bit of a Kleenex-tissue-week, and very sobering at times. Think how you might feel if you were at supper and one of them said, 'We are socially excluded, we haven't had a meal like this before where we all sit down and eat together.'

Reflection time could be very moving: They loved having candles (you can't have candles in hostels). One young man, holding a sponge ball, said: 'We must absorb everything that happens this week so that we can remember it back in Edinburgh.' Another, on being asked to talk about a favourite place, said: 'I haven't got one, all I know is care homes, disciplinary centres and prison.' – and yet that person entered into the life of Camas as much as, if not more than, any of the others. One person painted a picture of Camas with the island and cross, a kayak and an abseiler. One lad, who said he had no good memories before, now has – and sat with tears streaming down his face on the last evening.

After walking up the track on the last morning, we had a special Camas reflection, led by David, where a ball of wool was thrown across to each person with a spoken memory of the week. At the end of the reflection there was a web of wool and we were all connected, as we had been during the week. Then, because we were going our separate ways, the wool was broken and we wound bits around our wrists to remember our ties. (When I next saw the lads in Edinburgh they all had their wool around their wrists. 'We will never take it off, Viv, and can we go next year?')

Going back to Camas three weeks later I found ample evidence of the lads. If anyone stays in the larger dormitory, look up at the rafters. You will see 'Old Edinburgh Boys 2002' – they have left their mark.

Viv Davies, a member of the Iona Community

TEARS

Dance, calls the waves
but I will not dance.

Sing, calls the wind
but I will not sing.

Weep, sighs my soul
and I weep
and I dance
and I sing.

Jim Hughes, a member of the Iona Community

LOITERING WITH INTENT

Jesus was a loiterer. He stood with those who felt that God had rejected them, those who would say or feel that they were not worth God, those who had been told so by the religious and the pious ... Let us learn to loiter with Jesus in those ways and those places that he is least likely to be known. Even (perhaps especially) if we feel uncomfortable ...

Jesus loitered more with those whose lifestyle was not religious than with those who were. Jesus's example was not to build a holier-than-thou enclave but to loiter in places the powerful were scared to go.

Ewan Aitken, a member of the Iona Community

June 24

Community life is there to help us not to flee from our deep wound, but to remain with the reality of love. It is there to help us believe that our illusions and egoism will be gradually healed if we become nourishment for others. We are in community for each other, so that all of us can grow and uncover our wound before the infinite, so that Jesus can manifest himself through it.

Jean Vanier, L'Arche Community

June 25

During the darkest periods of history, quite often a small number of men and women, scattered throughout the world, have been able to reverse the course of historical evolutions. This was only possible because they hoped beyond all hope.

Brother Roger, Taizé Community

June 26
International Day in Support of Victims of Torture

I am a member of a small non-violent direct action group in Scotland, and some years ago we were all horrified by a TV programme which showed the export of electric shock batons from a factory in Glasgow to Saudi Arabia where they were being used for torture. We determined to use symbolic action to expose this trade to the local people of Glasgow as part of a campaign to bring the owner of the company to justice. Members of our group, using a cardboard template, spray-painted 'bloody' footprints going from the gates of the factory down to the traffic lights on the main street. When we came to court we had a sympathetic hearing and were given an unconditional discharge. Amnesty International and C.A.A.T. [Campaign Against the Arms Trade] raised the matter through the courts and eventually the owner was brought to trial and found guilty of illegal export of arms. Just one small victory.

It is such actions, however, which create the climate of opinion in which change can happen. Twenty years of Chile solidarity concerts, Amnesty International letter-writing campaigns, public meetings with refugees, films, books, talks and lectures all played their part in making the name of Pinochet so well known that when it came to the point of government decisions on extradition, there was already a huge groundswell of informed public opinion.

Helen Steven, a member of the Iona Community

Prayer

Almighty father, you sent your Son to bring the whole world the glorious liberty of the children of God. Open the eyes of the oppressor and the torturer to the blindness of their injustice. Open the way of freedom to those in prison for what they believe. Anoint us with your Spirit to make us servants of the oppressed and instruments of your power, so that justice and peace may embrace, and your love may rule in the hearts of all.

Amnesty International

June 27

Invisible we see You, Christ beneath us.
With earthly eyes we see beneath us stones and dust
and dross, fit subjects for the analyst's table.
But with the eye of faith, we know You uphold.
In You all things consist and hang together:
> The very atom is light energy,
> The grass is vibrant,
> The rocks pulsate

All is in flux; turn but a stone and an angel moves.
Underneath are the everlasting arms.
Unknowable we know You, Christ beneath us.

From a prayer by George MacLeod

June 28

God's word became human to accustom human beings to God.

Attributed to Ireneus of Lyon (2nd century)

June 29

CHRISTIANS SHOULD BE

Christians should be communities of loving defiance, not comfortable clubs of conformity.

Ron Sider

Christians should be without fear, happy, and always in trouble.

William Russell Maltby. Also attributed to Douglas V. Steere

RELEVANT THEOLOGY

When, after studying theology at New College, I went into industry as a manual labourer/pastor the move was met by contrasting reactions.

Some said, 'Marvellous. You are really identified with basic workers!'

I had to point out that my two degrees offered escape routes. The people I worked alongside had to take whatever work was available and make the best of it. 'I am not *identified*. I am only identifying as much as is open to me,' I told them.

Others said, 'You trained for ministry all that time; you could have been a theological educator – you turned your back on both!'

I answered this complaint, writing: 'This is not a rejection of ministry but a search for authentic ministry; this is not a rejection of theology but a search for relevant theology; this is not a rejection of scholarship but its completion.'

Ian M Fraser, a member of the Iona Community

Theology for the oppressed women, men and children in India is not an intellectual exploration. It is a daily struggle to understand the meaning of salvation in Christ from a place of alienation, exploitation and shame. It is a theology which aims at liberation through Christ who himself walks with the poor.

In a letter from a friend in India, from Peter Millar

July

Readings for Gay Pride Day

HOMOPHOBIA

I pray
that all those people
who think they have the right
to define what love is
and how we should love,
will one day be able
to see outside the cages
they have built around their hearts,
and accept me and my loving,
those whom I love
and am loved by.
Amen

Jenni Sophia Fuchs, a youth associate of the Iona Community

Leader:	For the quarter of a million homosexuals murdered in Nazi concentration camps, and those who remained imprisoned despite the Allied victory, and now live in history's closet:
ALL:	WE PRAY, O GOD, FOR THOSE WHO DIED IN CLOSETS.
Leader:	For millions of lesbians and gay men in countries in which there are no support systems or groups, in which revelation leads to imprisonment, castration or death:
ALL:	WE PRAY, O GOD, FOR THOSE WHO FEAR IN CLOSETS.
Leader;	For priests, nuns, ministers and lay church leaders

who, to serve the Church, cannot come out,
while bringing liberation to others who are oppressed:

ALL: WE PRAY, O GOD, FOR THOSE WHO LIBERATE FROM CLOSETS.

Leader: To all the colours of the rainbow
ALL: WE STAND WITH YOU WHEN WE ARE PERSECUTED.
Leader: To all the colours of the rainbow
ALL: WE CELEBRATE OUR DIVERSITY.
Leader: To all the colours of the rainbow
ALL: WE ARE WELCOME AT CHRIST'S TABLE.

Responses from a liturgy in Iona Abbey, 2000

July 2

'Even if apartheid could ever be constructed to be a just system of 'separate development' (a ridiculous and impossible idea) I would reject it as a Christian with all my being since its assertion that human love, friendship and sharing is impossible between people of different colours is a fundamental attack on God the creator.'

Trevor Huddleston to Iain Whyte, a member of the Iona Community

July 3

As a former social worker and informal support worker with experience working with people with severe learning disabilities or mental health challenges, I can do no less to honour the courage and shining human spirit of our differently-abled sisters and brothers than to cut through the crap and develop some more inclusive liturgies and worship resources that remind us we are all disabled in some way. It's just that our society values some disabilities over others, for example, amnesia among politicians or the total lack of a sense of the ridiculous among pop stars and other prima donnas.

Yvonne Morland, a member of the Iona Community

July 4

WESTERN CIVILISATION

Many tribal cultures and peasant societies lived and still live without war, without corruption, without pollution, without nuclear weapons, without population explosions, without exploitation, without drug abuse. And yet we call them poor and uncivilised, in need of 'development'. The Western ideology of materialism is teaching them to consider themselves poor and making them struggle to become rich. The rich show images, through advertising, which make people feel inferior, inadequate and deprived. It is like an unwritten conspiracy to undermine.

Satish Kumar

'Mr Gandhi, what do you think of Western civilisation?'

'I think it would be a very good idea.'

Mahatma Gandhi, in response to an interviewer in Britain during the 1930s

'Bombs are dropping while you're shopping!'

A chant heard on Princes Street in Edinburgh on a march to the American Embassy during the war against Iraq, 2004

THE WRITING ON THE WALL

I was hungry
and you formed a debating society to discuss it
I was imprisoned
and you just complained about the crime rate
I was naked
and you debated the morality of my appearance
I was sick
and you thanked God for your health
I was homeless and you preached to me
about the shelter of God's love
You seem so holy and close to God
But I'm still hungry, lonely, cold, and in pain
Does it matter?

Graffiti on a wall in New York City

A STORY OF HOPE
(From Iona)

An interfaith conference was held on the holy isle of Iona. From this a joint Moslem-Christian communiqué resulted in the decision that national interfaith services of reconciliation would take place. One would be in Edinburgh's St Giles Cathedral and the other in Glasgow Mosque.

But a problem arose with the Edinburgh event. The timing was going to clash with the Moslems' evening call to prayer. They would be unable to attend.

It was then that Dr Bashir Maan, the spokesperson for Glasgow Mosque, remembered something from the Hadith. This is the oral tradition of Islam. Seemingly Prophet Mohammed (peace be upon him) had allowed visiting Christians to use his mosque for their worship. Might it be conceivable, he wondered, for us likewise to do something in this spirit?

Scotland's Christian leaders responded warmly. They would even allow Moslem worship to be conducted in front of the altar at St Giles Cathedral as part of the service. So it came to pass that Christians watched on as Moslems prayed in their church. Our silence felt respectful to the point of inner participation.

The following week, on 25 October 1991, Imam Tufail Hussain Shah addressed Christians at prayer in the community hall of the Glasgow Mosque. Referring to the previous week's event, he said, 'We joined that night, and again now in this Mosque, to worship the same God, God as known to the early Jews as Yahweh. God as revealed in the Christian tradition through Jesus Christ. God whom we Muslims know by the Arabic word Allah … We share a common commitment to love, justice, charity, mercy, piety and peace. Building these qualities in our hearts perhaps matters more to God than cleverness in arguing about religion. I believe it is God, Allah, who has brought us together. Let us try to stay together and work for peace not only in the Gulf and Middle East, but throughout this planet, this universe of God.'

Some years later I was telling this story whilst lecturing in Edinburgh University. The son of a Nigerian imam came up to me afterwards. 'You know,' he told me, 'we read all about that in our newspaper in Nigeria.' He explained to me that at the time Moslems and Christians were killing each other in his country. His father and his colleagues were so astonished to hear that Scottish Christians could talk with Moslems that they decided to initiate the same approach with Christian leaders in their area. The killings did not entirely stop as a result, but they had greatly reduced.

Alastair McIntosh, a patron of the Growing Hope Appeal

July 8

PROSTITUTES AND TAX COLLECTORS

In Glasgow last week, a sixteen-strong immigration squad kicked down the front door of a house in Drumchapel at six in the morning, handcuffed the father, ransacked the home and removed a family, including children in their pyjamas, who had been living in Glasgow for five years, to a detention centre hundreds of miles away, without warning or preparation. The school friends of the family are devastated. In the present political climate, the distress of some Glasgow schoolchildren cuts little ice. But they are not stupid, these schoolchildren. They are enjoined to be tolerant, welcoming, anti-racist, and they have duly been all of these. What they see, however, is that politicians are actually dancing to a much more xenophobic tune. They are not practising what they preach. What they see is moral cowardice, a failure of integrity. They realise that high ideals are not really to be taken seriously after all. Cynicism grows, and the political process loses a little more of its future.

The political vocation (and I do believe it is a vocation) is perhaps the hardest one of all. It requires of often very idealistic and well-motivated people the recognition that they will have to act within iron constraints, that conflicting pressures will fatally undermine the integrity of means and ends, that an endless series of trade-offs and negotiations can still result in failure or worse, that however good the cause, violent means always produce violent outcomes which will mostly be borne by the innocent. So catastrophically unjust is our present dominant world order, so racist, so ecologically disastrous, so corrupt the global arms trade, that it is almost impossible to be politically engaged without being morally compromised.

And yet it *is* a Christian calling – to seek to improve the lives of our neighbours *and* our enemies alike, to try to do justice and make peace, to do what we can, not what we can't. Moral authority, says Paul, lies in recognising that the moral high ground (or faithfulness to God, we might call it) actually demands a different kind of equality with the sinners and outcasts, a solidarity in suffering that very few of us have the moral courage for. The best we can do is to have the humility to admit it, to abandon our claims to the moral high ground and to know that we will often find it in the last places we think to look. The prostitutes and tax-collectors (and it's probably worth noting that tax-collectors were hated not because they collected taxes but because they were considered to be traitors) for all the anti-social and dishonourable nature of their way of life, knew that they were doing the wrong thing, and believed in the other path. God is merciful even to us. But that's why the prostitutes and tax-collectors will be going ahead of us into the kingdom of God.

Kathy Galloway, from a sermon given at the Labour Party Conference in Brighton, 2005

BY GOD

'President Bush said to all of us: "I'm driven with a mission from God. God would tell me, *George, go and fight those terrorists in Afghanistan.* And I did. And then God would tell me, *George, go and end the tyranny in Iraq ...* And I did. And now, again, I feel God's words coming to me, *Go get the Palestinians their state and get the Israelis their security, and get peace in the Middle East.* And by God I'm gonna do it." '

George Bush, 2003, according to Nabil Shaath, Palestinian Foreign Minister

July 9

'You must criticise us. We will not like it. We will try to stop you. But it is your duty to keep on doing it.'

Julius Nyerere to the University of Dar-es-Salaam at the time of becoming Prime Minister of Tanganyika (now Tanzania)

From Iain Whyte, a member of the Iona Community.

July 10

SOME FACTS

Some facts about US, UK and world military spending:

In 2004 world military expenditure amounted to US$1035 billion, for the first time since the end of the cold war over one trillion US$.

In 2004 the USA spent US$466.6 billion on their military.

UK military expenditure amounted to US$54.4 billion = £29.9 billion.

(Statistics from the Stockholm International Peace Research Institute (SIPRI))

Think about how this money could have been used …

Hospitals
Nurses
Doctors
Finding a cure for AIDS
Finding a vaccine for malaria
Alleviating world poverty
'Third world' debt
Pensions
Schools
Youth centres
Sustainable energy
The arts
Music
Beauty …

Does it make you sad?
Does it make you angry?

Do you not believe it?

Think about this money being spent year after year
after year
after year …

Does it make you want to do something about it?

Neil Paynter

HEALING THE BLIND MEN

During the Gulf War of 1991, a vigil for peace was held at St Mary's Episcopal Cathedral in Glasgow and I vividly remember a prayer focused on the healing of the blind man (Mark 8:11–9:1):

'O Lord, spit on the eyes of Saddam Hussein,
spit on the eyes of George Bush,
spit on the eyes of John Major,
spit on our eyes,
take away our blindness,
give us vision and sight,
and a knowledge of the truth,
a deeper knowledge,
a saving knowledge,
lest we perish.'

Leith Fisher

WITH THE EYES OF THE HEART

I have heard of your faith in the Lord Jesus and your love toward all the saints, and for this reason I do not cease to give thanks for you as I remember you in my prayers. I pray that the God of our Lord Jesus Christ, the Father of glory, may give you a spirit of wisdom and revelation as you come to know him, so

that, with the eyes of your heart enlightened, you may know what is the hope
to which he has called you ...

Ephesians 1:15–18 (NRSV)

If we could only better recognise
that which is of God
in one another
and ourselves,
then our relationships would be
living icons and sacraments
of the overflowing mutual worship of the Trinity.

Jane Rogers, a member of the Iona Community, from a poem

July 13

We preach unconditional love in the church. I've learned the hard way that we
don't always receive it, we can't always give it, but those who have suffered
most are likely to be those who have the courage and the compassion to be
alongside the marginalised and the despairing. When we are hurting and
broken we often feel isolated and forsaken. When we are set apart by pain or
stigma it takes a special kind of person to pilgrim with us. But when that does
happen, we experience the giving and receiving of the vulnerable love that
following Christ's way is all about.

Kate McIlhagga, a member of the Iona Community

Can desolation
invite me to rediscover
the sacred in myself
and in the world?

Peter Millar

SUSTENANCE

'What sustains you?'
we've been asked,
in a small group of people,
more strangers than friends.

Can you tell me
what makes your heart leap?
What makes your soul sing?
What keeps you believing?
What keeps you breathing?

For me, this is not a question
I can answer casually
or ponder lightly.
You see,
there are times when I am close to the edge,
drunk from memories of fists in my flesh
and haunted by darkness and screams of death threats;

it's not a question I can embrace easily,
but I know I wake now with the light warming my face;
I wake now with laughter in my heart;
I stop and notice with just one breath
that life is for living and I smile at death
so I can tell you what sustains me …

it's the sun caressing my skin
and the moon playing on the sea
it's the feeling after Liverpool win
and praying as I plant a baby tree
it's Fiona's laugh
and Michelle's fragility
it's soaking in my bath
and Neil's creativity
it's eating beans we've grown from seed
and Isobel dancing with her drum
it's walking with millions who believe in peace
and watching daft films purely for fun
it's 'Hallelujah' sung by K.D. Laing
and Alice Walker's words of healing,
it's the gentle love of Thich Nhat Hanh
and loving my body and simply feeling
it swimming and cycling with the wind in my hair
and little Iona Mary pulling me near
it's sharing and trust, and freedom and care …

it is simply this:
living and life
loving and love

Rachel McCann

NO ONE CAN TAKE YOUR PLACE

The symphony needs each note
The book needs each word
The house needs each brick
The ocean needs each drop of water
The harvest needs each grain of wheat
The whole of humanity needs you
as and where you are
You are unique
No one can take your place.

Michel Quoist

So you begin … I begin.
I picked up one person –
maybe if I didn't pick up that one person I wouldn't have picked up 42,000.
The whole work is only a drop in the ocean.
But if I didn't put one drop in, the ocean would be one drop less.

Mother Teresa

CAMAS REFLECTION

Give me some more of these silences
The kind that are filled with the sounds of creation
Like the constant ebb and flow of the sea
Or directionless noise of the wind and rain
Or the solitary cry of the oystercatcher, echoing against granite.

Give me some more of these silences
The kind that just hang in timeless security,
enabling the mind to drift into uncharted places
So comforting, so reassuring – the moment never needs to end.

Give me some more of these conversations
Like the ones I've had along the track,
by the sink, in the garden, round the fire,
building boxes, sewing tents, painting signs, digging earth.

Give me some more of these conversations
The kind that help gain understanding,
break down barriers, challenge assumptions
The kind that inspire me to move beyond conversation, into action.

Give me some more of this friendship
The kind that allows me to be vulnerable
Valued, accepted for who I am
Away from familiar constraints and expectations –
where an idea is quashed, maybe goes unnoticed.

Give me some more of this friendship
The kind where a hug is never far off

And tea for twenty is never much hassle
Where there's plenty of music and singing and laughter
Yet where raw edges can't be ignored.

Give me some more of this simple lifestyle
Where wholesome food, heart-pumping exercise
and pure, clean air just make so much sense.

Give me some more of this simple lifestyle
Where the absence of comforts like electricity, hot water and flush toilets
doesn't really matter
Where all our rushing around, work deadlines,
heavy meetings and stressful phone calls
seem so unimportant.

This simple lifestyle frees the mind, lifts the spirit,
gives space to think, relaxes my body, feeds my creativity,
gives life a new perspective.

Give me some more of this life together
Where, in this special place,
so small, so secluded,
yet so connected to the world,
we find a spiritual meaning in the rhythms of our day

Give me some more of this life together
Where the depth of our relationships
is carried in our hearts
And our experiences go beyond this place
to inspire us and challenges us
and fill us with hope.

Neil Squires, a member of the Iona Community and a volunteer at Camas, the Iona
Community's adventure centre on the Isle of Mull

THE PRAYER STOOL

I leave aside my shoes
– my ambitions,
undo my watch
– my timetable,
take off my glasses
– my views,
unclip my pen,
– my work,
put down my keys
– my security,
to be alone with you,
the only true God.

After being with you,
I take up my shoes
to walk in your ways,
strap on my watch
to live in your time,
put on my glasses
to look at your world,
clip on my pen
to write up your thoughts,
pick up my keys
to open your doors.

Graham Kings

If we desire a society based on equality, democracy and the end of social divisions then we must live lives which express these values.

Bob Holman

The power of God is capable of finding hope where hope no longer exists and a way where the way is impossible.

Attributed to Gregory of Nyssa (2nd century)

'I dream of a day when there will be bread in every mouth, a smile on every face and a rose in every hand.'

Tawfiq Zayyad (1932–1994), when Mayor of Nazareth, in a conversation with Norman Shanks, a former leader of the Iona Community.

NEVER DOUBT

The only thing necessary for the triumph of evil is for good people to do nothing.

Edmund Burke (1729–1797)

Never doubt that a small group of thoughtful, committed citizens can change the world. Indeed it is the only thing that ever has.

Margaret Mead

Today I shall dream –
of people together,
loving, sharing, eating, dancing.

And at the end of the day,
when things are much the same,
I shall continue to hope.
I shall remember that the personal
is always political; that inner peace
cannot be separated from wholeness
and health in community;
that small acts of beauty
by small groups of people
still carry the potential
to change the world.

Joy Mead, a member of the Iona Community, from a longer poem

July 22

Practise random kindness and senseless acts of beauty

Fridge magnet

In the midst of hunger and war
WE CELEBRATE THE PROMISE OF PLENTY AND PEACE.

In the midst of oppression and tyranny
WE CELEBRATE THE PROMISE OF SERVICE AND FREEDOM.

In the midst of doubt and despair
WE CELEBRATE THE PROMISE OF FAITH AND HOPE.

In the midst of fear and betrayal
WE CELEBRATE THE PROMISE OF JOY AND LOYALTY

In the midst of hatred and death
WE CELEBRATE THE PROMISE OF LOVE AND LIFE.

In the midst of sin and decay
WE CELEBRATE THE PROMISE OF SALVATION AND RENEWAL

In the midst of death on every side
WE CELEBRATE THE PROMISE OF THE LIVING CHRIST.
AMEN

Edmund Jones

The wilderness and the dry land shall be glad,
the desert shall rejoice and blossom;
like the crocus it shall blossom abundantly,
and rejoice with joy and singing.

Isaiah 35:1–2a (NRSV)

July 24

If you are prepared to risk everything, you can do anything.

The actress Patricia Routledge, in a TV interview, 1998

July 25

Jesus is a friend who walks in when the world walks out.

Bumper sticker

July 26

THE SHEPHERD AND SHEEP

In my Reformed tradition (the Church of Scotland identifies itself as 'Catholic and Reformed'), the image of the shepherd and sheep has been only too powerful. To take another image, 'The minister' has been thought of rather like the axle of a wheel which is always at the centre of things and holds everything together. Services are most often one-man-band or one-woman-band affairs with the congregation dumbed down or given minor parts to play. This is in sharp contrast to a service in the early church described in 1 Corinthians 14:26–33 which is marked by the full participation of members. Paul does not try to thwart that building up of worship from the congregation as a whole. He simply insists that it must be orderly. Moreover, he starts not with an 'if you should meet this way' or 'when you might meet in this way'; he uses the word *hotan* – 'every time you meet …', indicating that the normal form of worship is fully participatory.

Go to worship in Iona Abbey. The service might be led by a professor of theology, or a cook, or a gardener, or a housekeeper or a maintenance man.

Ian M Fraser, a member of the Iona Community

GOD'S PEOPLE

Last Saturday I sat in the Abbey at the welcome service. It was being led by a young woman member of the resident group, with the assistance of other young staff and volunteers. None of them was clergy, none theologically trained, none even on the programme staff. She led a full abbey in worship with such grace, dignity, warmth and sensitivity that I was profoundly moved. The commitment, attention to detail and depth of participation that the service allowed was a model of teamwork by a group of people who had just put in a full and demanding week's work of heavy physical labour. But what struck me most was not just the content, but the integrity of message and medium. In the leadership of God's people in worship with such authority there was a powerful visible sign that God's image is equally to be seen in someone young, female, non-professional, and so we really believe that all are made in God's image … In the confident leading of singing, of praying, of breaking open the Word by such very young people there was a palpable sense of empowerment. I came away from the service confident that the Spirit still has work for us to do on Iona.

Kathy Galloway

Worship needs to be for the people, by the people, with the people, about the people.

Anon

July 27

LIGHT FILLING MY LIFE: A MEDITATION

There is a yogic exercise which encourages the practitioner to imagine that with each in-breath you breathe in light which begins at the top of the spine and travels downwards. With each out-breath that light is then sent to every corner of the body. As the meditation continues so the light continues to soak the spine, coursing its way to each bodily extremity. In my varied attempts to pray, to communicate with God, to enhance my listening capabilities and to be open to receive light from God, this exercise helps. The image of light filling my life is one that gives me hope and courage.

Ruth Harvey, a member of the Iona Community

July 28

THE TRUTH

I remember that in my evangelical youth I was given a folding chart. It explained in diagrammatical form what various (Christian) 'heretical' groups believed about the main doctrines. Then at the end was a column headed 'The Truth' and all you had to do was to run your finger down the column to find 'The Truth'. How easy! How convenient! Hinduism didn't even make it onto the chart! (Bye bye, Gandhi. Tough you didn't even make it.)

What South India did for me was to help me to say a formal bye bye to any vestiges of that attitude, and also to face some other questions. I discovered that I have abandoned any belief in 'Christianity' and Christendom. Let me explain what I mean by that. I believe in Jesus Christ, incarnate, crucified and risen. I believe He is the Lord, the light of the world. And I believe in God the Father, and in the presence of the Creator Sprit. I believe in humanity. To all the rest, I hang loose. Questions about who or who cannot celebrate/receive Communion, who is in or out, about priestliness, etc, are not even remotely interesting …

Ron Ferguson

July 29

'What is the deepest meaning of Buddhism, master?' The Master made a deep bow to the pupil.

A Buddhist saying

July 30

'… Get thee glass eyes,
And, like a scurvy politician, seem
To see the things thou dost not.'

William Shakespeare, from *The Tragedy of King Lear*, Act 4, Scene 5

How unlike the North American woodland Indians we are. They often think in terms of the consequence of their actions upon the seventh unborn generation. Contemporary life is geared to the length of political office.

Ghillean Prance, Science Director of the Eden Project (Cornwall), and former Director of Royal Botantic Gardens, Kew

We do not inherit the earth from our parents.
We borrow it from our children.

Native American saying

* Note: Nuclear waste from nuclear power plants (plutonium) remains dangerous for 25,000 years. (Ed.)

August

August 1

We need to recognise the persistence and place of conflict in human history. We are not here to avoid conflict but to redeem it. At the heart of our faith is a cross ...

Robert Runcie, former Archbishop of Canterbury

August 2

WINGS OF PRAYER

Your peaceful presence, giving strength,
Is everywhere,
And fallen men may rise again
On wings of prayer.

Benedictine Nuns of Stanbrook Abbey, from *The Stanbrook Abbey Hymnal*

August 3

EXPLORERS, NOT MAP MAKERS

Following Jesus does not mean clinging to an idea or holding on to a principle. It is walking the path of one who gave his life for his friends and called his followers to do the same.

Henri Nouwen

Christ is a person to be trusted, not a principle to be tested. The Church is a movement, not a meeting house. The faith is an experience, not an exposition. Christians are explorers, not map makers.

George MacLeod

August 4

Hope is believing in spite of the evidence – and watching evidence change.

Jim Wallis, Sojourners Community

August 5

Thou shalt know Christ when he comes,
Not by any din of drums,
Nor the vantage of his airs,
Nor by anything he wears,
Neither by his crown
Nor by his gown –
But his presence known shall be
In the holy harmony
That his coming makes in thee

Anon, 15th century

THE SUN BEHIND ALL SUNS

Children of the atomic age can never forget that it was on the day of the Feast of the Transfiguration, 6 August, 1945, that the first atomic bomb was dropped on Hiroshima. Eyewitnesses spoke of a flash 'brighter than a thousand suns'. There could be no sharper posing of the question, 'Which power do we in reality worship and follow?' Is it that power which harnesses the forces of God's world for blind and indiscriminate destruction, in which human beings are 'wasted', reduced to shadows on the pavement? Or is it the power of the One who shines on the mountain top, the One whom our Celtic ancestors called 'the Sun behind all suns', in whom our humanity is glorified?

Leith Fisher, a member of the Iona Community

Prayer

O Sun behind all suns,
I give you greeting this new day.
Let all creation praise you.
Let the daylight
and the shadows praise you.
Let the fertile earth
and the swelling sea praise you.
Let the winds and rain,
the lightning and the thunder
praise you.
Let all that breathes,

both male and female, praise you.
And I shall praise you.
O God of life,
I give you greeting this day.

J. Philip Newell

BY WHAT POWER?
(Acts 4:5–12; 1 John 3:16–22)

In the story of Acts, Peter and John, members of a minority religious faction, hauled in front of the high priests for preaching to (and converting vast numbers of) a local Jerusalem crowd, are asked: 'By what power or by what name did you do this?'

The crucial question in the trial is not why did you do this? or what were your motives? or even who was paying you? but: by what POWER? and in whose NAME? Power and names. The greatest threat to the authorities at that time was an unknown power and a name, the name of Jesus Christ, that converted thousands.

By what power, and in whose name do you, do we, live our lives today? Are we held captive by the powers of consumerism, globalised marketing and 'keeping up with the Joneses'? Do we put great store by the name on our designer labels, by the image that we present to the world, by aligning ourselves with the prestigious and powerful? Or do we have deeper, more subtle, more compelling allegiances that orientate our lives around a spiritual truth? These are pressing, existential questions which are relevant not only to Christian believers, to the

Peters and Johns of today, but also to thinking, morally questioning, spiritually seeking people throughout our nation and beyond. What motivates us? What beliefs do we firmly hold on to? For what or for whom would we put ourselves on the line? By what power, in whose name, do we act?

Ruth Harvey, a member of the Iona Community, from a sermon

August 8

The power of love is greater than the love of power.

George MacLeod

August 9
Nagasaki Day

ENOUGH NUCLEAR WEAPONS TO DESTROY THE WORLD TEN TIMES OVER

There is surely an inherent racism right at the heart of the beliefs that are fuelling this war. In our total obsession to rid Saddam Hussein of every last vestige of a weapon of mass destruction, whether chemical, biological or nuclear, we are content to draw a veil of hypocritical secrecy over the fact that we have enough nuclear weapons to destroy the world ten times over, we are still carrying out experimentation into biological warfare at Porton Down in England, and it was from his Western allies that Saddam obtained the chemicals for the gas he used against the Kurds. Loud protests are made about India,

Pakistan, North Korea being in breach of the Non-proliferation Treaty, but the Treaty also calls for the states already in possession of nuclear weapons to act 'in good faith' with utmost urgency towards 'real and genuine disarmament'. In fact the next generation of nuclear weapons beyond Trident is already being planned and paid for.

Helen Steven, a member of the Iona Community

'I die with the conviction, held since 1968 ... that nuclear weapons are the scourge of the earth; to mine for them, manufacture them, deploy them, use them, is a curse against God, the human family and the earth itself.'

Phillip Berrigan, founder of the Ploughshares Movement, shortly before his death in 2002

August 10

I want to beg you to be patient towards all that is unsolved in your heart and try to love the questions themselves. The point is, to live everything. Live the questions now. Perhaps you will gradually, without noticing it, live along some distant day into the answer.

Rainer Maria Rilke

August 11

THE SOURCE OF LIFE

For times when we no longer trust that our poverty and our need of each other is a source of life, Lord, have mercy.

From a liturgy by *da* Noust

(*da* Noust is an informal circle of members and friends of l'Arche Edinburgh. The word noust is Orcadian for a boat shelter on the shore, a place to withdraw for rest and renewal, prior to setting out fishing once more in the morning. L'Arche is an ecumenical community welcoming adults with learning difficulties, assistants and others to a shared life.)

August 12
International Youth Day

THE FEELING OF SOLIDARITY WAS IMMENSE

My concern at the way Tony Blair seemed to be following George Bush in an unstoppable determination to go to war with Iraq fired me to go to London on Saturday, 15th February to join in the largest march for peace that had ever been held in Britain. It was the second demonstration I had attended, the first being the peace march in September last year.

I went by train, which gradually filled up with people and banners as we got nearer London. It was an encouraging feeling and the conversations between strangers flowed freely. We joined thousands of others of all ages and backgrounds, but we were united in our desire to stop war with Iraq.

To be marching with over a million people was a moving experience. The crowd was peaceful but very vocal with people shouting, singing and dancing to the variety of bands who interspersed the crowds. Many people waved banners with imaginative slogans such as 'Make tea not war' and 'Tony walk with us not the US'. We walked three miles in an incredible 4 hours, eventually reaching Hyde Park where the march spread out to fill most of the park. There were speeches from eminent people including Jesse Jackson, Tony Benn, Bianca Jagger and Charles Kennedy. Around the world another 60 countries had similar marches taking place and messages were read out to the crowd from Palestine and Rome, where 2 million Italians had gathered to protest against the impending war. The feeling of solidarity was immense.

Hannah Kenyon, a youth associate of the Iona Community

August 13

SOLIDARITY

Solidarity is usually thought of as a political term, and is often used very sloppily in the West. It often means 'I am in sympathy with'. But as an active and not a passive word, the response to such statements as 'I am in solidarity with the oppressed people of South Africa', 'with the revolution in Nicaragua', or 'with the poor of this country' must always be, 'How?' How are we in solidarity?

Kathy Galloway

Most of us recognise that we cannot live on bread alone, although we must continue to walk in solidarity with those who have no bread at all.

Peter Millar

Solidarity is the tenderness of peoples

From Nicaragua

August 14

BEING FAITHFUL

I remember a conversation I once had with a woman from the Greenham Common Peace Camp. She had spent a week in the Abbey on Iona, in rest and recreation after two years of continuous and intense pressure, strain and physical demand. Her 'home' had been destroyed countless times. She had been in court and in prison, she had been subjected to harassment and abuse. But she had a great week on Iona and obviously felt restored by it, ready to go back to Greenham. As we were standing together on the jetty waiting for the ferry, she said to me, 'You know, I'd love to be doing what you are doing.' (At the time I was warden of the Abbey.) 'I think it is really important.' I was amazed, because I felt very humble in the presence of someone who had so much put her whole life out there on the front line. I said to her, 'I feel exactly the same about what you are doing. I've so often felt that I should be there at Greenham, but haven't because of my children and other things.' There and then we agreed that each of us did what we did, not just on our own behalf but on behalf of each other. I did what I did on Iona to the best of my ability for her because she couldn't be there; she did what she did at Greenham to the best of her ability for me because I couldn't be there. Although we were engaged in different forms of action, we were in solidarity with one another – and with all the other people who were being faithful on our account in *their* situations. That conversation, and that sense of mutual accountability, kept me going more than anything else during the hard times on Iona – that she needed me to be her representative on Iona, just as I needed her to be mine at Greenham.

Kathy Galloway

TIME TO REST AND RECUPERATE
Exodus 23:10–11; Leviticus 19:9–10

As I read these passages from the books of the law I think of the experience of the Aymara Indians in the highlands of Bolivia. In that tribe, individual families own areas of land, but it is the community that determines what will be grown for the benefit of all. Each land owner is told what crop to grow, and is regularly instructed to leave an area fallow. This communal organisation of agriculture ensures that an adequate diversity of crops, such as potatoes, quinoa and oca, are grown to meet community requirements. It also gives the land time to rest and recuperate. If a family's land is to be fallow for a year, the produce of other members of the tribe will take care of all needs. As a result the Aymara agricultural system has functioned for hundreds of years without destroying the soil.

Ghillean Prance, Science Director of the Eden Project (Cornwall), and former Director of Royal Botantic Gardens, Kew

Man – despite his artistic pretensions, his sophistication, and his many accomplishments – owes his existence to a six-inch layer of topsoil and the fact that it rains.

Author unknown

August 16

PLACE, BELONGING AND FOOTBALL PITCHES

For most of us, community means those we live amongst, but there's more to a community than the people alone. The place itself is of equal importance. Every one of us needs a sense of place, a sense of belonging somewhere.

But many Scots are blocked from belonging fully to the land that is Scotland.

Too often a TV up a high rise is a person's only window on nature.

Just one thousand rich landowners control nearly two thirds of private Scottish land.

Yet there's enough of Scotland to average 4 acres for everyone – that's three football pitches each!

Alastair McIntosh, a patron of the Growing Hope Appeal

August 17

I love to tell the story! 'Twill be my theme in glory
To tell the old, old story of Jesus and His love.

Arabella Katharine Hankey (1834–1911)

August 18

No one can make a greater mistake than to do nothing because they think that the little they can do will have no effect.

Anon

If you think you are too small to make a difference, try sleeping with a mosquito.

African proverb used by the Dalai Lama

I NO LONGER BELIEVE THAT

There was a moving story told at Santiago de Compostela during the most recent Faith and Order Conference. One of the bishops of the Church of South India described how a Hindu friend came frequently to his church. On one occasion he came forward at the Eucharist. The bishop, somewhat startled, gave him the elements and later sought him out to explain what communion meant. A few weeks later, the man came back and again presented himself at the altar. With rather more misgivings, the bishop again gave him bread and wine, but afterwards said, with some indignation, 'Did you not understand what I said? To share this meal you have to make a commitment to the Lord Christ. You are a Hindu. You have not made that commitment.' To which the Hindu replied, 'When I read your Scriptures, I find that the Jews did not have to stop being Jews to love and follow Jesus. Why do I have to stop being a Hindu?' The force of that question was, for the bishop, revelatory.

Clearly, there is more similarity in many ways between Judaism, Christianity and Islam in terms of scriptural heritage and religious style, than between the three of them and the faiths of Far-Eastern origin. But it is precisely because, in Christian tradition, there *can* only be one God, that we have to give some account of that God's relation to the whole inhabited earth – the Buddhists, the Sikhs, the Pagans, the Baha'i, the agnostics, the humanists, the unlabelled people who live a day at a time with whatever crops up: birth, death, family conflict, good times, bad times.

The scenario as portrayed for much of Christian history has been that God's relationship to all these communities is one only of judgement, and of a call to repentance; never of support and endorsement.

I no longer believe that.

Elizabeth Templeton

August 20

THE GOSPEL

A way of life that disregards and damages God's creation, forces the poor into greater poverty, and threatens the right of future generations to a healthy environment and to their fair share of the earth's wealth and resources, is contrary to the vision of the Gospel.

From the Catholic Church in England and Wales

Prayer

O glorious God, the whole of creation proclaims your marvellous work; increase in us a capacity to wonder and delight in it, that heaven's praise may echo in our hearts and our lives be spent as good stewards of the earth; through Jesus Christ our Lord. Amen

Reverend Christopher Irving

Almighty God, Creator:
the morning is yours, rising into fullness.
The summer is yours, dipping into autumn.
Eternity is yours, dipping into time.
The vibrant grasses, the scent of flowers,
the lichen on the rocks, the tang of seaweed.
All are yours.
Gladly we live in this garden of your creating.

George MacLeod, founder of the Iona Community, from a longer prayer

Every spring
I leave seed-heads
on my kingcup
in hope that one day
they will germinate.

Today, in the seventh autumn,
I notice a new young plant
growing
at the far side of the pond.

Margaret Lyall

August 23

LOVE

We are all bastards, but God loves us anyway.

Will D. Campbell

And You are love: uncalculating love.
When we kick You in the teeth,
Your sole concern is whether we have stubbed our toes.

George MacLeod, from a prayer

August 24

WHAT MORE WILL IT TAKE?

Stand first at the foot of the Cross, where you will find your companions are women (the men, according to Scripture, having all turned and fled). Then stand at the empty tomb on Easter morning, and again according to Scripture you will hear the risen Christ address Mary Magdalene and say to her, 'Go to my brothers and tell them – tell them I am about to ascend to my Father.' There is here a clear Apostolic Sucession – women witnessing to the death and resurrection of Christ. What more will it take to persuade you?

Mary Levison, in an address to the General Assembly of the Church of Scotland, 1998

You are witnesses of these things.

Luke 24:48 (GNB)

What I find in the Bible – which differentiates our faith from all other world religions – is precisely that *God is to be found in the material*. And that He came to redeem man, body and soul. The gospel claims the key to all material issues is to be found in the mystery that Christ came in a body, and healed bodies and fed bodies, and that he died in a body, and rose in a body: to save man body and soul.

George MacLeod

Leader:	Christ has no hands but our hands;
ALL:	NO HANDS BUT OUR HANDS
	TO DO GOD'S WORK IN THE WORLD.
Leader:	Christ has no lips but our lips;
ALL:	NO LIPS BUT OUR LIPS
	TO PROCLAIM THE GOOD NEWS.
Leader:	Christ has no love but our love;
ALL:	NO LOVE BUT OUR LOVE TO SHARE
	WITH THE IMPRISONED, THE SILENCED, THE PERSECUTED,
	THE HARASSED, THE MARGINALISED.
	AMEN

From a justice and peace service in Iona Abbey
Responses adapted by Neil Paynter from a prayer attributed to St Teresa of Avila.

Spirituality is what you do with your body about God.

David Coleman, a member of the Iona Community

August 26

God of the dispossessed,
show me how I can be in touch
with people like Cheikh Kone (of the Ivory Coast)
who is now without a home
because he spoke the truth.

Peter Millar, a member of the Iona Community

August 27

Solvitur ambulando: it is solved by walking.

Latin proverb, sometimes attributed to St Augustine

Blessing

Bless to us, O God,
the earth beneath our feet.
Bless to us, O God,
the path whereon we tread.
Bless to us, O God,
the people whom we meet.

Celtic blessing

We are not called to be fearful, we are called to love;

We are not called to be perfect, we are called to be faithful;

We are not called to be fearless, we are called to be obedient;

We are not called to be all knowing, we are called to believe;

We are not called to claim, we are called to give;

We are not called to be victorious, we are called to be courageous;

We are not called to lord it over others, we are called to serve.

For it is in serving that we shall reign;

it is through courage that we shall find victory;

it is by giving all that we shall gain all;

it is in believing that we shall find certainty;

it is in obedience that we shall overcome;

it is in faithfulness that we shall find perfection;

it is in loving that we shall dispel all fear;

it is in surrendering to Christ that we shall become the hope of the world;

it is in slavery to Christ and his justice that we shall find freedom;

now and forever, for ourselves, and for the world.

Alan Boesak, from a speech in 1989

CREDO

Today has been a restless day
things going wrong in all directions
and my anger rising
at others
at my circumstances
at myself.

God, you are in the midst of this
I sense your presence
prowling like a tiger
pushing me
pursuing me
restless yourself until I change.

I am ready to let rip
to hurl stones into oceans
to pound my fists into a brick wall.
I am ready to shout
to rip sheets into shreds
to curse the darkness
to bury my head into warm flesh and sob.

I am afraid, God,
that there is no one here but you and me
my friends are out or busy or far away.
Do I trust you enough to give you my anger, my loneliness?

Do I believe you enough to reach through the emptiness
and grasp for your hand?

Credo
God, I love you,
I can say no other words.

Ruth Burgess, a member of the Iona Community

GAZE ON HIM

People are always thinking that conduct is supremely important, and that because prayer helps it, therefore prayer is good. That is true as far as it goes; still truer is it to say that worship is of supreme importance and conduct tests it. Conduct tests how much of yourself was in the worship you gave to God. You get the most help from religion when you have stopped thinking about your needs, even for spiritual strength, and think about God. Gaze and gaze on Him; let us then try to recall to ourselves something of the majesty of God.

William Temple, from Keith Patrick Cardinal O'Brien, a patron of the Growing Hope Appeal

'There is meaning in the search.'

Peter Millar, at an annual gathering at Burndale, Kilmartin, Scotland

September

September 1

Set our hearts on fire with love to thee, O Christ,
that in that flame we may love thee
and our neighbour as ourselves.

Eastern Orthodox prayer

September 2

Achievement is not what you've got – it's what you've overcome.

Anon

'Very truly, I tell you, the one who believes in me will also do the works that I do and, in fact, will do greater works than these, because I am going to the Father. I will do whatever you ask in my name, so that the Father may be glorified in the Son. If in my name you ask me for anything, I will do it.'

John 14:12–14 (NRSV)

September 3

'HOW MANY BAGS OF RICE TODAY?'

This is revolution; this is resurrection. So often the little, brave symbolic actions we make seem so futile, pathetic and downright stupid. At the age of 48 still to have no house of one's own, no adequate pension scheme, to be paid below the tax level – ridiculous. 'You were demonstrating 30 years ago,' say my friends, 'when will you grow up?' Going to prison for planting potatoes inside a sub-marine base – now that is really crazy. I am convinced that we are called to take action, to live the Kingdom now, and that if we do that faithfully to the utmost of our being, *that* is already the power for change. Not for us to see the result, only to believe in the power of resurrection.

There is a story of the Fellowship of Reconciliation (FOR) in the United States in the '50s when the Cold War with China was at its hottest. There was a terrible famine in China and FOR urged its members to send little bags of rice to President Eisenhower to persuade the US government to send food aid rather than engage in war. Hundreds of thousands of bags were sent daily from individuals from all over the States. Eventually the fighting reached such an intensity that the Pentagon was pressing Eisenhower to use nuclear weapons on Quemoy and Matsu. The President turned to his aides and asked, 'How many bags of rice today?' and on hearing the answer ruled out the possibility of nuclear weapons in the face of such concern. These people never knew.

Helen Steven, a member of the Iona Community

Prayer

Forgive us, Lord Jesus, for grain mountains and milk lakes
while stomachs are empty.
Forgive us for political and economic systems
which depend on the weak getting weaker and the rich possessing the earth.

David Jenkins, from *The United Reformed Church Prayer Book*

A VISIT TO PALESTINE AND ISRAEL, 2002

It was good to be there, although the situation was grimly depressing (and has deteriorated since). Nevertheless, I came away feeling more positive than I was before going. I am not sure why, but chiefly because there was still shared with us faith and endurance and hope. I am very grateful for receiving these gifts … But now, as what is happening there goes on and on and lessens in news value, I am more convinced than ever that we will fail if we just look on from a distance. We are all involved there. I hope the programme for prayer vigils and other means to keep the people there in our hearts goes well. That goes hand in hand with whatever people can do, boycott or any other means of sticking their necks out. We should not go quietly into this dark night.

Colin Morton, a member of the Iona Community and former minister of the Church of Scotland congregation in Jerusalem

The world belongs to God
THE EARTH AND ALL ITS PEOPLE
How good it is, how wonderful
TO LIVE TOGETHER IN UNITY
Love and faith come together
JUSTICE AND PEACE JOIN HANDS
If Christ's disciples keep silent
THESE STONES WOULD SHOUT ALOUD
Open our lips, O God,
AND OUR MOUTHS SHALL PROCLAIM YOUR PRAISE

From *Iona Abbey Worship Book*

QUOTES FROM YOUNG PEOPLE AT CAMAS:

'It is a safe place and we can be free. We don't have to carry knives like we do back home. People treat us with respect. I can relax and have a laugh, learn new things and do things I didn't think I could do.'

'This is our spiritual home where we can be free to be who we are without the fear and prejudice of the city.'

'I have learned that I am a valuable person who can contribute and care for others. I have felt accepted and like I belong.'

QUOTES FROM PEOPLE ON IONA:

'I liked the way all the different religions came together. The world would be a better place if everybody could be like that.'

'I didn't smoke as much, not because I had to go out to the hut, but because I didn't feel the need.'

I didn't have to take as many pills. It was so peaceful there. Everybody went out of their way to make us welcome.'

September 6

A PARABLE

It was a chilly, overcast day when the horseman spied the little sparrow lying on its back in the middle of the road. Reining his mount he looked down and inquired of the fragile creature, 'Why are you lying upside down like that?'

'I heard the heavens are going to fall today,' replied the bird.

The horseman laughed. 'And I suppose your spindly legs can hold up the heavens?'

'One does what one can,' said the little sparrow.

Source unknown

September 7

The fact that things change and move and flow is their life. Try to make them static and you die of worry.

George MacLeod

'Therefore I tell you, do not worry about your life, what you will eat or what you will drink, or about your body, what you will wear. Is not life more than food, and the body more than clothing? Look at the birds of the air; they neither sow nor reap nor gather into barns, and yet your heavenly Father feeds them. Are you not of more value than they? And can any of you by worrying add a single hour to your span of life? And why do you worry about clothing? Consider the lilies of the field, how they grow; they neither toil nor spin, yet I tell you, even Solomon in all his glory was not clothed like one of these. But if God so clothes the grass of the field, which is alive today and tomorrow is thrown into the oven, will he not much more clothe you – you of little faith? Therefore, do not worry, saying, 'What will we eat?' or 'What will we drink?' or 'What will we wear?' For it is the Gentiles who strive for all these things; and indeed your heavenly Father knows that you need all these things. But strive first for the kingdom of God and his righteousness, and all these things will be given to you as well.

'So do not worry about tomorrow, for tomorrow will bring worries of its own. Today's trouble is enough for today.'

Matthew 6:25–34 (NRSV)

September 8

ROOT CAUSES

One of the most vital aspects of attempting to discern the truth is to seek the root causes of the conflict. In 1972 I was working with a Quaker protest project in Vietnam. My initial involvement arose out of a somewhat naïve altruistic desire to 'do something' about the war. Working in orphanages we may have done a little bit to alleviate suffering, although nothing more than the Vietnamese could do, but the main lesson I learned was that the best way of helping the Vietnamese people was to go back home and tackle the real causes of their suffering by campaigning to end the war. This search for the root causes involves engaging with the complexities of the military industrial nexus, and exposing them in ways that bring clarity. During the Gulf War, for example, a German highlighted the connection with Western dependence on oil reserves by chaining his Volkswagen out on his own front lawn with a huge placard saying 'The real cause of the war'. Dramatic and symbolic changes of lifestyle can also help to highlight the causes of oppression and focus on our own or our government's part in oppressive regimes. Placing the blame where it really lies saves us from an easy complacency.

The Quaker John Woolman said: 'May we look upon our treasures, the furniture of our houses, and our garments, and try whether the seeds of war have nourishment in these our possessions.'

Helen Steven, a member of the Iona Community

September 9

IN THE NAME OF GOD

For all those who turn their backs on me,
who call me abnormal, or disgusting,
or other hurtful things in the name of God,
and who pray for my demons to be cast out,
I pray in return that they may never have to
feel the hurt,
the pain, the fear and anxiety,
which I suffer from their actions;
that their demons, too, be cast out,
and that together
we can turn our minds
to putting an end to fear and hatred,
in the name of God.
Amen

Jenni Sophia Fuchs, a youth associate of the Iona Community

DEMON POSSESSION

The issue of demons invites us to face up to the questions, 'What are the forces that keep us and our world in bondage?' 'What makes us less free and able for the service of God and one another?'

Take an example of one contemporary demon of enormous destructive power, racial prejudice. None of us is untainted by that demon, one which prevents us from loving our neighbour fully. How do we deal with this demon, confront it and cast it out? First, we need to become more self-aware, more self-critical about how we respond to people face to face, and how we respond to events around the world. We begin by acknowledging the plank in our own eye. We continue by approaching the religion, values and culture of others with openness, humility and a willingness to learn. We eschew hasty judgements. We freely acknowledge our ignorance and partiality.

We must also recognise that the struggle with racial prejudice is not only an inner, personal battle. There is also a war raging in society at large. Here we have to pick our ground and tactics with care. On one hand, it is no good simply blaming folk for attitudes picked up unthinkingly from their upbringing and environment. Here in Britain we still struggle with perverse attitudes of superiority inherited from the old days of the British Empire, from which we need to pray to be delivered. It's no good blaming people but equally it is not right to continue tolerating a destructive spiritual force, which is what racial prejudice is, in us and in our society. Here is a force which destroys and diminishes people, tears them apart from one another, colonises their minds, legitimates many forms of oppression and exploitation. There is a war to be fought, beginning with ourselves, in the name and following the example of Jesus, against contemporary demons which bind and estrange and render worthless. Racial prejudice is only one demon; there are plenty of others around.

Leith Fisher, a member of the Iona Community

September 11

The language of threat and the logic of war breed violence. As long as the cries of those who are humiliated by unremitting injustice are ignored, terrorism will not be overcome.

Konrad Raiser, former head of the World Council of Churches

The greatest terrors of this world are hunger, poverty and deprivation, which kill hundreds and thousands of people every day.

In a letter from Bangladesh, sent to Norman Shanks, former leader of the Iona Community

September 12

The one supreme conviction that I cannot get away from and – without any dramatics – am quite willing to die for is that only the spiritual can mould any future worth having for the world.

George MacLeod, in a sermon from Iona Abbey

September 13

With those who would kill themselves
to kill others
WE PRAY FOR PEACE
With those who want to build up
their nuclear weapons
WE PRAY FOR PEACE

With those who want to inflict
terror and fear
WE PRAY FOR PEACE
With those who want war
WE PRAY FOR PEACE

Rosie Miles

September 14

HOPE FOR YOU AND ME

Hear this true story of an Indian boy whose father was rich with vast estates and many gardeners.

The boy was a little wretch. At twelve he pinched the gardener's pittance of a wage, to buy himself cigarettes.

At fourteen he pinched a gold nugget from an elder brother and blamed a gardener, who got the sack and went to live in the village, which meant starvation.

At sixteen, not surprisingly, he tried to commit suicide but had not the guts even to do that.

At seventeen his father fell desperately ill. Horrified, the boy felt consumed by guilt, seized a bit of paper and wrote it all down, all the above and yards more dirt confessions. 'You must read this, father.' He said: 'You must know what I am really like,' expecting at best a tongue lashing.

But the father read it, crumpled it up, burst into tears, and said, 'I forgive you.' That was all.

The name of the boy? Mahatma Gandhi. Who became the spiritual ruler of India.

So there is hope for you and me, twisters though we continue to be … if only we will accept the Father's word and be up and doing, NOW.

George MacLeod

September 15

A READING FOR RAMADAN

About the middle of Ramadan 2000 I sit talking with a Muslim widow from Pakistan. The door opens and in comes a girl; she is almost twelve. She is in a school uniform: trousers, shirt and blazer. Her hair is tucked into a baseball cap. She dumps her heavy school bag on a chair and climbs the stairs two at a time.

She is the youngest of four children, born three weeks after her father's sudden death. She is a friendly, confident and articulate child who has become a friend. One day, at the age of six, she took my hand, saying, 'Come and see what these white people have done to us.' Every bit of glass in their second-hand car had been smashed with heavy bricks.

In ten minutes she comes downstairs, transformed, wearing a pale yellow shalwar and qamiz, her long black hair loose over her shoulders. She is barefoot. She sits down on the carpet, warming her hands at the gas fire and smiles at her mother and me. 'Is the food ready to open the fast?' she asks her mother. She is typical of many Asian children trying to cope with living within two cultures. I am suddenly moved to ask if she feels British. 'Course I'm British. I was born here. I speak English. I get on with most white people.'

Stanley Hope, a member of the Iona Community

September 16
International Day for the
Preservation of the Ozone Layer

GRASS ROOTS

The earth mourns and withers,
the world languishes and withers;
the heavens languish together with the earth …

Isaiah 24:4

Don't leave climate change to the experts. It is a simple issue, it affects us all, and it is only because of our silence that the carbon economy remains so powerful. So, don't leave it to someone else; speak about climate change. Grassroots public pressure could be our only chance of saving the planet.

From *The Ecologist*

JESUS CHRIST IS WAITING

Jesus Christ is waiting,
waiting in the streets;
no one is his neighbour,
all alone he eats.
Listen, Lord Jesus,
I am lonely too.
Make me, friend or stranger,
fit to wait on you.

Jesus Christ is raging,
raging in the streets,
where injustice spirals
and real hope retreats.
Listen, Lord Jesus,
I am angry too.
In the Kingdom's causes
let me rage with you.

Jesus Christ is healing,
healing in the streets;
curing those who suffer,
touching those he greets.
Listen, Lord Jesus,
I have pity too.
Let my care be active,
healing just like you.

Jesus Christ is dancing,
dancing in the streets,
where each sign of hatred
he, with love, defeats.
Listen, Lord Jesus,
I should triumph too.
Where good conquers evil
let me dance with you.

Jesus Christ is calling,
calling in the streets,
'Who will join my journey?
I will guide their feet.'

Listen, Lord Jesus,
let my fears be few.
Walk one step before me;
I will follow you.

John L. Bell & Graham Maule

Whoever wants to serve me must follow me, so that my servant will be with me where I am. And my Father will honour anyone who serves me.

John 12:26 (GNB)

DOERS OF THE WORD

I expect to pass through this world but once;
any good thing therefore I can do, or any kindness that
I can show to any fellow creature, let me do it now;
let me not defer or neglect it
for I shall not pass this way again.

Stephen Grellet (1773–1855)

But be doers of the word, and not hearers only, deceiving yourselves. For if any one is a hearer of the word and not a doer, he is like a man who observes his natural face in a mirror; for he observes himself and goes away and at once forgets what he was like. But he who looks into the perfect law, the law of liberty, and perseveres, being no hearer that forgets but a doer that acts, he shall be blessed in his doing.

James 1:22–25

Prayer

Help me to be a doer and not just a hearer or a speaker.

Ralph Morton

September 19

PRAYER

I thank thee, God, for knowing me better than I know myself, and for letting me know myself better than others know me. Make me, I pray, better than they suppose, and forgive me what they do not know.

Attributed to Abu Bakr (573-634), the prophet Mohammed's father-in-law

September 20

I believe in getting in hot water. It keeps you clean.

G.K. Chesterton

Wash yourselves clean. Stop all this evil that I see you doing. Yes, stop doing evil and learn to do right. See that justice is done – help those who are oppressed ...

Isaiah 1:16–17 (GNB)

Lord, teach us to see our world
as your love would make it;
a world where peace
is built with justice
and justice is guided by love.

Let our wrestling
with your truth
bear fruit in this world
and bring your kingdom closer.
Amen

From the Common Daily Prayer of Dominican Peace Action

VISION

Where there is no vision, the people perish.

Proverbs 29:18 (King James Bible)

We know that we perish if we don't have enough food or rest, that is obvious; we even know that we need beauty or something in us withers – but vision? Yet without vision to follow there is no purpose to life, and our spirit is impoverished. I sometimes wonder if the binge drinking, the attraction to drugs in countries where people have all their basic needs met, and more, is because people have no vision, no purpose in life, despite all the affluence and comfort. To follow a vision, to live the dreams deep within you, can be alarming, exciting, life-giving and exhausting, but you are fully alive.

Prayer

Your will, O God, be done.

Not mine, with my desire for safety,
for comfort, and anything for a quiet life.

Your will, O God, be done.

Not mine, which gets so mixed up
with fear and anger, and those wayward
hurt feelings.
And wishes, Lord –
mixed up with wishes is my will.
For pleasure, for wealth – to win, to succeed,
for my family to be happy.

Bring my will in line with Yours.
My will alongside Yours.
So that when I say,
'Your will be done.'
It is mine too.

Chris Polhill, a member of the Iona Community

IN THE HEART OF GOD

'Do not fear, for I have redeemed you;
I have called you by name, you are mine.
When you pass through the waters, I will be with you;
and through the rivers, they shall not overwhelm you;
when you walk through fire you shall not be burned,
and the flame shall not consume you …
Because you are precious in my sight,
and honoured, and I love you.

Isaiah 43:1–4 (NRSV)

and the Great Spirit who loves us
and has given us our true names
whispers them in the darkness
when we are alone
when we are weary
when we are despairing
and we are re-membered
in the heart of God.

Kathy Galloway, from a poem

September 24

ENRICHED BEYOND MEASURE

As I write, Ramadan is here once again and another year has flown. Dialogue, I have learned, is much more than the dead end where the concentration on theology often leads. It brings friendship, which in turn leads to understanding and trust. It is a permanent state in which imagination, trust and courage can grow and which makes action on social justice possible. When we know and trust each other I have often been surprised at what it becomes possible to discuss and do together. Strangely enough, in many of our meetings and conversations the teaching of Jesus has come alive.

In Muslim people I have found friendship, kindness, hospitality, generosity, respect for others, a deep sense of humanity and compassion and a concern for justice. I remain grateful that my life has been enriched beyond measure. It has been a journey that I would not have missed for anything.

Stanley Hope, a member of the Iona Community

September 25

This world is too small and too crowded and too interdependent for us to indulge our incapacity to cope with difference.

John Rackley, a member of the Iona Community

Readings for Buy Nothing Day

LIVE SIMPLY

Try to live simply. A simple lifestyle freely chosen is a source of strength. Do not be persuaded into buying what you do not need or cannot afford.

From Quaker Advices and Queries No. 17

What did we bring into the world? Nothing! What can we take out of the world? Nothing! …

Timothy 6:7–8

Prayer

Lord, may I live simply
so that others
may simply live.

Adapted from a quote attributed to St Elizabeth Ann Seton (1774–1821). This quote is also sometimes attributed to Mahatma Gandhi.

A conversation overheard on the train from Lanark to Glasgow, early one Monday morning:

Younger man: So, did you go to the pub on the weekend then?

Older man: No. I never go to the pub any more. The pub is pish. Pish ... Before you used to go to the pub and people would tell you stories. You know, tell you what they'd done and where they'd been ... Now all they ever tell you is 'I got this' and 'I bought that'. It's pish – there's no stories any more.

Prayer

God, help us to store up on earth things that truly matter –
love, friends, experience, precious moments ... life in all its fullness.

Help us to spend our lives meaningfully
and to have something real to show for it at the end.

God, thank you for storytellers, entertainers, comedians, writers ...
For people who make us laugh, bring us closer, give us understanding,
give us hope;
for people who open up to us the absurdity,
wonder and mystery of being human.

Thank you for the stories in the Bible and for the characters there.
Thank you for Jesus, and for the stories he told.

Neil Paynter

What I kept I have lost. What I gave, that I have.

Sydney Carter

DAUGHTERS OF EVE

'A woman who insists on becoming a contemporary Daughter of Eve refuses to corset her body and repress her emotions to conform to some model of perfection. Instead she frees her voice from the endless strictures and behavioural norms which have silenced her for so long. As a Daughter of Eve I refuse to be nice any longer, to be apologetic because I have physical and intellectual imperfections. I celebrate what I have in common with my sisters, but I also celebrate what it is that sets me apart, and this very apartness, this insistence on difference, should be enough, paradoxically, to enable me and all Daughters of Eve to celebrate each other's beauty and uniqueness – rather than allow a patriarchal model of perfection to divide us from each other.'

The artist Joyce Gunn Cairns, from the catalogue of her exhibition, Daughters of Eve

September 30

Amazing grace! (how sweet the sound!)
that saved a wretch like me!
I once was lost, but now I'm found,
was blind, but now I see.

John Newton (1725–1807)

October

The bodies of grown-ups
come with stretchmarks and scars,
faces that have been lived in,
relaxed breasts and bellies,
backs that give trouble,
and well-worn feet:
flesh that is particular,
and obviously mortal.
They also come
with bruises on their hearts,
wounds they can't forget,
and each of them
a company of lovers in their soul
who will not return
and cannot be erased.
And yet I think there is a flood of beauty
beyond the smoothness of youth;
and my heart aches for that grace of longing
that flows through bodies
no longer straining to be innocent,
but yearning for redemption.

Janet Morley

GRANDMOTHERLY GOD

Grandmotherly God,
we thank you for the table of your generosity around which we are gathered:
for the turning of the seasons and the fruitfulness of the earth;
for the extended family to which we belong.

Grandmotherly God,
we praise you for your quiet wisdom and experience of life:
for your knowledge of us and faithfulness to us over the years;
for your ability to surprise us, and for the twinkle in your eye.

Grandmotherly God,
we thank you for your long-suffering and unquestioning love:
that you have put up with years of being taken for granted;
that you have borne us upon your heart when you have been far from ours.

Grandmotherly God,
you understand us better than we imagine.

Forgive our impatience, our self-preoccupation, our selfishness.
Restore our unity and our true sense of identity,
and all for your love's sake.
Amen

Richard Sharples, warden of Iona Abbey
This prayer was used in a service in the Abbey.

October 2

Everything begins in mysticism, and ends in politics.

Charles Peguy (1873–1914)

Spirituality is the place where prayer and politics meet.

Kate McIlhagga, a member of the Iona Community

October 3

Even the simplest poem
May destroy your immunity to human emotions.
All poems must carry a Government warning.
Words can seriously affect your heart.

Elma Mitchell

October 4
St Francis Day

BLESSING

May God bless you with discomfort at easy answers, half-truths, and superficial relationships, so that you may live deep within your heart.

May God bless you with anger at injustice, oppression, and exploitation of people, so that you may work for justice, freedom and peace.

May God bless you with tears to shed for those who suffer from pain, rejection, starvation and war, so that you may reach out your hand to comfort them and to turn their pain to joy.

May God bless you with enough foolishness to believe that you can make a difference in this world, so that you can do what others claim cannot be done.

And the blessing of God, who Creates, Redeems and Sanctifies, be upon you and all you love and pray for this day, and for evermore. Amen

Fourfold Franciscan blessing

October 5
International World Teachers' Day

CROSSING FRONTIERS

Ten young people in Lima, Peru, who had trained as teachers and could have been upwardly mobile, decided to live in a deprived community. They put down their roots into the life of the people, accepted their culture, learnt their key words and used these to encourage the development of awareness of their oppressed situation and to encourage choices for freedom.

Four of the teachers took on paid employment. The $72 per month earned by the four had to support the total team and pay for teaching materials as well.

They crossed a financial frontier, adopting a simple style of living which allowed the income of a few to do for all. Thus they found an alternative to that of financing by outside agencies.

They crossed an educational frontier, immersing themselves among those who had little education or none, honouring their wisdom, enlarging it. They crossed a class frontier, refusing the status available to middle-class professionals, choosing rather to live alongside those who were regarded as belonging to the lowest stratum of society. They crossed a cultural frontier, deliberately refusing to be cultural capitalists; deciding to honour the culture of the lowly rather than the prestige culture for which they could have opted. They crossed a frontier of individualism, for they acted as a team. Four of them came to meet me to make it clear that leadership does not fall to any one of them, but is shared.

Read Matthew 19:28–30.

Ian M Fraser, a member of the Iona Community

October 6

SWARAJ*

I will give you a talisman. Whenever you are in doubt, or when the self becomes too much with you, apply the following test. Recall the face of the poorest and weakest man whom you may have seen, and ask yourself if the step you contemplate is going to be of any use to him. Will he gain anything by it? Will it restore him to a control over his own life and destiny? In other words, will it lead to *swaraj* for the hungry and spiritually starving millions? Then you will find your doubt and yourself melting away.

Mahatma Gandhi

* Freedom, self-rule

WE MUST BE HUMAN

Is not this what our congregational life in the main requires? How often are church social activities de-humanised; either straining after a false piety so that it is a relief for everyone (in their hearts) to get away, or so indistinguishable from the multitude of sub-human secular fellowships about, that we might as well have stayed at home.

Some of us remember the first fortnight of the Community in 1938, when a group composed of parsons and craftsmen found themselves pledged to live together The Faith, as applied not to leisure hours but to the whole round day. It was a terrific strain! ... They were in a 'religious community' so they must be different: walk softly; mention no conceivable subject on which anyone might with passion differ; laugh moderately, after full assurance that it was a laughing matter; and act more generally as if some grapeshot had lodged in their spine and never been removed. Only a row could clear such artificiality. And after it we became a community of very ordinary men, who knew it, said it, and thereby began to grow. Only with such a fellowship can God do anything at all.

The thing is a parable. Our congregations miss the zest of the early Christian Church because we have forgotten the glorious emancipation of our true humanity that was the Incarnation. Jesus the carpenter, the friend of shepherds and of fishermen, showed us God by being human – and in three days set at nought the complex Temple that was forty years in building. He made risen humanity His Temple. We must be human.

George MacLeod, 1962

I sometimes think that people leave behind the actual richness of their humanity when they get into church. Should it not be the other way round?

Dorothy Millar, an associate of the Iona Community and former member of the resident group on Iona, who died in 2001

October 8

IN THE FLESH

Lord Jesus, it's good to know
that you lived in the flesh;
walked where we walk, felt what we feel,
got tired, had sore and dirty feet,
needed to eat, and think about
where the next meal was coming from.

But it's even better to know
that you enjoyed your food,
the feel of perfume on your skin,
the wind on your face, a child in your arms
and the good wine at the wedding.

You didn't mind when people touched you,
even those who were thought of as unclean.
You kissed people with diseases
and laid your head on your friend's shoulder.
Thank you for understanding our bodily pains and pleasures
and for valuing them.

Kathy Galloway

Readings for Columbus Day

HOLOCAUSTS

An Amerindian has written to me, expressing his anger: 'To us, Hitler killing six million people was not the world-shaking event it was to Europe, from our vantage point of having over forty million indigenous people killed by Europeans, of having whole nations of Indians completely destroyed.'

Prayer

We remember native Indians, their land intruded on, whole nations wiped out, their customs and cultures devalued and destroyed.

We pray for international action to protect and cherish these ravaged cultures, and to honour their gentle relationship with the world around.

Ian M Fraser

Creating community which is inclusive of people who face many differing challenges in their physical, emotional, spiritual and mental health is as urgent a matter of social justice as redressing the polluting of our planet, eradicating nuclear weapons, participating fully in our political processes. It is not about pretending that we can be a therapeutic community in a clinical sense. It is about welcoming people who are already in our midst. People who are disenfranchised from contributing many gifts because they are seen as problems, as embodiments of their particular medical condition or perhaps, more honestly, as mirroring wounds and frailties which we fear in ourselves now or for the future.

Many of these people, in coming to terms with, for instance, physical weakness, erratic movement, impaired concentration, have had to learn to carry the cross of their discipleship more deeply, more honestly, with more dignity than many of us manage or try to do. And sadly, because of our refusal to be inclusive as a society, they often have to do it alone.

Yvonne Morland, a member of the Iona Community

But we have this treasure in earthen vessels, to show that the transcendent power belongs to God and not to us. We are afflicted in every way, but not crushed; perplexed, but not driven to despair; persecuted, but not forsaken; struck down, but not destroyed; always carrying in the body the death of Jesus, so that the life of Jesus may also be manifested in our bodies. For while we live we are always being given up to death for Jesus' sake, so that the life of Jesus may be manifested in our mortal flesh. So death is at work in us, but life in you.

2 Corinthians: 4:7–12 (RSV)

October 11

Wise, mysterious God,
give us the faith to pray
For all that has been – thanks
For all that will be – yes! *

Beautiful, surprising God,
give us light to pray
For all that has been – thanks
For all that will be – yes!

Risk-taking, dancing God,
give us courage to pray
For all that has been – thanks
For all that will be – yes!

Immanent, incarnate God,
give us peace to pray
For all that has been – thanks
For all that will be – yes!

Penniless, pilgrim God,
give us cheerfulness to pray
For all that has been – thanks
For all that will be – yes!

Disturbing, sheltering God,
give us justice to pray
For all that has been – thanks
For all that will be – yes!

Holy, liberating God,
give us love to pray
For all that has been – thanks
For all that will be – yes!

By Ruth Burgess, Kate McIlhagga, Margaret Stewart, members of the Iona Community

* Lines three and four in each stanza adapted from a prayer in Dag Hammarskjöld's
  Markings

THE FIRST STREAM WE CROSSED

Before I visited the Maku Indians on the upper Rio Negro in Brazil, I had read about their fish poisoning festivals where they catch a huge number of fish, using plants which stun them, and have a large feast. After spending a few days with the Maku I finally persuaded the chief to allow us to take part in such a fishing expedition. He said it would not be in the nearby stream but another one a short walk through the forest. After a two-hour walk, which at the Indians' pace is a jog, we came to a stream which appeared ideal for fishing, but the chief said it was not this one. Two hours later the next inviting stream was crossed, but again the fishing was not to be there. In spite of their heavy loads of the particular plant they were going to use for fishing, the Indians trotted on through the forest until eight hours later we reached the designated spot on a stream that looked exactly like the four or five we had already crossed. The botanists were exhausted, but the Maku immediately set about the business of building a small log bridge over the stream, and placing their leaves of the spurge plant, *Euphorbia cotinifolia*, on it. This plant has chemical which react with the gill-membranes of the fish and cause them to become asphyxiated and float to the surface. While the men beat the leaves with sticks to allow the sap from the plant to fall into the river, some of the women stirred up the mud upstream, whilst others began to gather up the stunned fish downstream … They collected a huge amount of fish reminiscent of the bounty when the resurrected Jesus advised his disciples to cast their net on the other side of the boat … When I asked Chief Joaquim why we could not have fished at the first stream we crossed, he replied that they had fished there a few months ago, and that each of the other streams we crossed had been fished within the period of the last twenty moons. He said, 'If we fish like this in a river more than once in twenty moons there will be no fish left.'

Ghillean Prance, Science Director of the Eden Project (Cornwall), and former Director of Royal Botantic Gardens, Kew

Only when the last tree has died
and the last river has been poisoned
and the last fish has been caught
will we realise that we cannot eat money.

19th-century Cree Indian

October 13

God is not only the God of Abraham, Isaac and Jacob, but of Tom, Dick and Harriet, though they might not know it.

Jim MacEwan, a member of the Iona Community

October 14

Let nothing disturb you,
Let nothing dismay you,
All things pass,
God never changes.

St Teresa of Avila

But you are the same,
and your years have no end.

Psalm 102:27–28 (NRSV)

October 15

A BLESSING FOR A WORK DAY

May God bless you
as you manage your work,
as you take painful decisions.
May God bless you
as you relate to others,
and give you strength for the day ahead.

Kate McIlhagga

October 16
World Food Day

O God, to those who have hunger give bread,
to us who have bread
give hunger for justice

A grace from Central America

No matter how poor they were, the people I met were still singing, singing human dignity.

Father Joseph Wresinski (1917–1988), founder of ATD Fourth World

What I believe can be summed up in five words: God is love; people matter.

Stewart McGregor, a member of the Iona Community

KINGDOM

It helps now and then to step back
and take the long view:
the kingdom is not only beyond our efforts,
it is even beyond our vision.

We accomplish in our lifetime only a tiny fraction
of the magnificent enterprise that is God's work.
Nothing we do is complete,
which is another way of saying
that the kingdom always lies beyond us.
No statement says all that could be said.
No prayer fully expresses our faith.
No confession brings perfection.
No pastoral visit brings wholeness.
No programme accomplishes the Church's mission.
No set of goals and objectives includes everything.

This is what we are about.
We plant the seeds that one day will grow.
We water seeds already planted,
knowing that they hold future promise.
We lay foundations that will need further development.
We provide yeast that produces effects
far beyond our capabilities.

We cannot do everything,
and there is a sense of liberation in realising that.

This enables us to do something,
and to do it well.
It may be incomplete, but it is a beginning,
a step along the way,
an opportunity for the Lord's grace to enter
and to do the rest.
We may never see the end results,
but that is the difference between
the master builder and the worker.

We are the workers, not the master builders,
ministers, not messiahs.
We are the prophets of a future not our own. Amen

Words drafted by Ken Untener for Cardinal Dearden
(This prayer is sometimes called 'The Prayer of Oscar Romero'.)

THE KINGDOM

It's a long way off but inside it
There are quite different things going on:
Festivals at which the poor man
Is king and the consumptive is
Healed; mirrors in which the blind look
At themselves and love looks at them
Back; and industry is for mending
The bent bones and the minds fractured
By life. It's a long way off, but to get
There takes no time and admission
Is free, if you will purge yourself
Of desire, and present yourself with

Your need only and the simple offering
Of your faith, green as a leaf

R.S. Thomas

From Alison Elliot, ex-Moderator of the Church of Scotland and a patron of
the Growing Hope Appeal

Prayer

O God, you have set before us a great hope
that your kingdom will come on earth,
and have taught us to pray for its coming:
make us ready to thank you for the signs of its dawning,
and to pray and work for the perfect day
when your will shall be done on earth as it is in heaven.
In the name of Jesus Christ.
Amen

From *Iona Abbey Worship Book*

October 20

I have never understood why one Christian would want to have more than
another.

The late President Julius Nyerere of Tanzania

From Jim MacEwan, a member of the Iona Community

A PRAYER OF THANKS FOR HEALING LOVE

She came, Lord, to my bedside,
a nurse of tender years,
younger than my granddaughter,
a mere slip of a girl.
She came, Lord, to me,
aged and frail,
sick and weak,
and I doubted what she could do for me.
She touched, Lord, with tender hands
my wrinkled skin and bony frame,
with gentle skill
and knowing look.
She touched, Lord, my life with love –
beyond my weakened body,
she reached my very soul.
She healed, Lord, my broken life,
my furrowed brow,
my wasted muscles tensed with pain,
my sullen look,
my very face turned away from any gaze.
She healed, Lord, and gave me time
to learn again to take and not reject such tender love.
She healed, Lord,
and gave me hope.
She loved, Lord,

she loved even me,

the me of such frailty and brokenness

such dying and hopelessness

that I doubted whether anyone could love,

whether I could love, whether You could love.

She came, Lord, and she loved me as I am.

She came, and touched, and healed, and loved,

and went away

that others, too, might know.

Tom Gordon, chaplain of Marie Curie Hospice in Edinburgh and a member of the Iona Community

October 22

ONE WORLD WEEK

Imagine shrinking the earth's population to a village of 100 people
with all the existing human ratios remaining the same.
The village would have 61 Asians, 12 Europeans, 13 North or South Americans,
13 Africans. One person from Oceania.
There would be 51 females and 49 males.
70 non-whites, 30 whites.
70 non-Christians and 30 Christians.
50% of the village's wealth would be in the hands of 6 people –
all North American citizens.
80 villagers would live in substandard housing;

70 villagers would be unable to read;
while 50 would suffer from malnutrition.
One villager would have a college education.

Statistics used by many international aid organisations, from the 'Global Village e-mail'

O God, You are One – make us one.

A prayer used in India

October 23

Having asylum seekers in our congregation has made us more acutely aware of the contexts in which people are suffering in other parts of the world. It has given us as a congregation the opportunity to share with people in ways that would not have previously been possible.

Ian Galloway, a minister in Glasgow and a member of the Iona Community

In Britain, racism is a denial of our democratic tradition. But for Christians, racism denies the unity and solidarity of all humanity which is at the heart of the gospel. We have a choice: to do nothing, or to take up the challenge.

Stanley Hope, a member of the Iona Community

October 24

TREADING ON THE FACES OF THE POOR

Long years ago this writer was close to the depression in the shipyards of Govan in the 1930s. At one time nine out of ten shipbuilders were unemployed. The symbol of the enemy was the 'bloated capitalist' with white waistcoat, frock coat, gold watch chain, rakish top hat and flaunted cigar 'treading on the faces of the poor' … Not enough folk grasp that the issue has been projected on the world stage. It is all of us, collectively in the West, who wear the waistcoat, top hat and flaunted cigar.

George MacLeod, 1989

October 25

How can I be with the poor when I am unwilling to confess my own poverty?

Henri Nouwen

October 26

HOSPITALITY AND GENEROSITY

While I was a teacher in Lesotho I felt a huge responsibility to the students I was teaching, because I have been given so much throughout my education, and I felt it was only right that I tried my hardest to give as much as I could to them that would help them in any way. I did give a lot to them – but it was nothing compared to what I was given in return. We were welcomed into their society and really made to feel as though we belonged, which helped us through the difficult times (of which there were many). I feel a debt of gratitude to all the friends I made there because of all they have taught me, often unknowingly, which has made me truly appreciate the opportunities I have been given in life, and how many people who have almost nothing really appreciate what they do have, without always wanting more.

During our stay, we were fortunate enough to be invited to several students' homes, which was an eye-opening experience. To see a large family living in two rooms the size of my living room, without electricity, running water or much money, being welcomed as one of them, and given a meal which could easily have cost a week's wages, was a truly humbling experience. When so many people in Britain are so reluctant to share anything, despite being able to afford it, it seems amazing to me that people who literally have almost nothing are so keen to share what little they do have, and feel offended if we (who have more than enough) do not accept their offer of hospitality and generosity. It was a time of my life I will never forget, and I will undoubtedly have to return one day.

Alice Kan, a former Iona Community volunteer

October 27

THE GOSPEL OF CHRIST IS COURAGEOUS

A church that doesn't provoke any crisis, a gospel that doesn't unsettle, a word of God that doesn't get under anyone's skin, a word of God that doesn't touch the real sin of the society in which it is being proclaimed – what gospel is that? Very nice, pious considerations that don't bother anyone, that's the way many would like preaching to be ... The gospel of Christ is courageous; it's the 'good news' of him who came to take away the world's sins.

Oscar Romero

October 28

TWISTERS

The Bible, corporately presented, is the evolutionary account of how the power of non-violence can be seen as the true nature of things. Christ, says the Revelation of St John, was crucified before all worlds. Suffering Love was God's nature from the start.

What a book it is! All the great characters are twisters! (That should make it relevant for our day!) Abraham was a twister. So was Jacob. So was David (a direct forebear of Jesus). So certainly were James and John, trying to get the seats on Christ's right and left hand at the Last Supper, when the Kingdom, still seen by them in the materialist sense, seemed immediately at hand. The seat on the right hand and the seat on the left (in an Eastern court) is where you hand out the perks, distribute the juicy jobs, and rake in the commission. The other disciples were furious that the two brothers had got in first with the request! No wonder Jesus thereupon went to Gethsemane to pray, till his sweat turned to blood, that his sacrifice might be postponed. 'Dear God,' he said, in effect, 'despite two years in my company, my disciples haven't got a clue what it's all about. If it be possible, let this cup pass till the ship has a dependable crew.'

To grasp this is further to close the credibility gap about the practice of non-violence. This new solution of power is not just for the rarefied few. It is offered as possible conduct here and now to twisters like the present writer and like you the present reader.

George MacLeod

For the word of God in scripture,
For the word of God among us,
For the word of God within us,
Amen

From *Iona Abbey Worship Book*

October 29

Karl Barth said we should pray with our Bibles in one hand and the daily newspaper in the other.

Leith Fisher, a member of the Iona Community

October 30

'Justice and peace will not be achieved through military power and the use of violence.'

Norman Shanks, speaking at an anti-war rally in Glasgow, 2001

The war horse is a vain hope for victory, and by its great might it cannot save.

Psalm 33:17 (NRSV)

THE ONLY PLACE TO BE

For so many folk in and out of the church, the parish is still seen as the only proper place for ministry and being a minister is fundamentally a parish experience.

Yet it is that kind of narrow, 19th-century perspective that will be the death of the church. It allows many congregations to be holy huddles. It places power in the hands of the few and disempowers the people who want to truly be the church. And it allows people outside the church to write it off as being irrelevant. Some folk in the church criticise those of us who want to make the faith relevant, rooted in the real world. For me, that is the only place to be. Jesus spent more time in the streets and on the hillsides than he ever did in the synagogues and the institutions. My decision to walk the political path is a reflection of my faith in a kingdom of justice and freedom, the lifting up of the poor and the liberation of the oppressed. It is not an add-on or an extra; my faith remains at the heart of what I do.

Ewan Aitken, a member of the Iona Community

November

November 1
All Saints' Day

Saints authenticate themselves. The idea that the church can authenticate saints should be seen as a nonsense. It results in a distortion of the whole idea of sainthood ...

Saints are a company of people who are trying to live Jesus Christ's way, set apart from the world but for God in the world, to companion Christ in its trans-formation. They need not be highly distinguished or prominent, though being so does not exclude them. In the parable of the Last Judgement in Matthew, their marks are justice and compassion, not religious conformity ...

[Saints are] that rag, tag and bobtail army of believers who face up to life in the strength and name of Jesus Christ, who, if they are found wanting at any point, pick themselves up, dust themselves down and soldier on with humour and grace. This and that side of death a great cloud of witnesses cheer us on and give us heart. They are the saints of God, not many known to those who take it upon themselves to authenticate saints officially!

Ian M Fraser, from a reflection

They serve at check-outs, empty bins,
They teach, and make and mend;
They feed the hungry back from school
The victimised defend;
To voiceless folk they lend an ear
And immigrants befriend.

Ian M Fraser, from the song 'The Saints of God'

I recently conducted the funeral of a 32-year-old wife and mother who died in our hospice. She was the most delightful woman, and had a wonderful husband, good family support, and two lovely little children. As part of her funeral service her husband asked me to read out something he had written, a personal reflection on what he had learned as he and his wife faced illness and the prospect of death. It was a brave thing to offer in public his personal thoughts. But he believed it to be right. With his permission I quote part of what he wrote, and you will see, with me, how right he was.

If I've learned any lessons from this tragic and painful few months it is that life itself is very fragile and one shouldn't assume that they will automatically live a long life. Make the most of life because you never know when it will be taken away from you – live life to the full every day – not just occasionally. If you love someone, tell them so and don't assume they know, because one day a time will come when they won't be there to tell any more.

Tom Gordon, chaplain of the Marie Curie Hospice in Edinburgh and a member of the Iona Community

Prayer

If it be your holy will, tell them how we love them, and how we miss them, and how we long for the day when we shall meet them again.

George MacLeod, from a longer prayer

THE COURAGE TO SAY NO

Somewhere along the line, the word 'No' has to be uttered in the name of a greater 'Yes'. We are called to be peace-makers, and that is a tough business. It is certainly not about being peace lovers (isn't everybody?) or about being passive-ists. The biblical word for peace – shalom – is a rich concept, involving right relationships with God and human beings. It is a tough, disciplined notion, not to be dispersed in the sentimental twanging of guitars. It is peace-with-justice, and it is cross-shaped ...

To say 'No' in today's world in the name of a greater 'Yes' is hard to do alone. It requires communities of resistance, with prayer at their heart.

Ron Ferguson

THE COURAGE TO SAY YES

We live in a world which sets value by market forces and whose spirituality is one of value addition, of extrinsic worth. So it is good news to say yes to and to practise Jesus's gospel of *intrinsic worth*, in which all living things, including the earth itself, have innate value separate from and beyond their utility; in which the commodification, the selling, of all life is resisted and reversed and in which justice is done. To be human in Jesus's way is *to act justly*.

We live in a world of seemingly hostile global forces, of the sense of powerless-ness to effect positive change which results in ethnic conflict and resource wars and of the collapse of traditional support structures. So it is good news to say yes to, and to practise, not de-personalised but *re-personalised human relation-ships*, and inclusive respect for the 'other' (neighbour *and* enemy) and new structures of care for the weakest in which the potential of all people, not just 'our people', can be protected. To be human in Jesus's way is *to love kindness.*

We live in a world in which human pride, *hubris,* which thinks of itself as creator rather than created, has come to threaten life on earth. So it's good news to say yes to and to practise a more *self-disciplined ethos of reverence and respect* for cultural, spiritual and bio-diversity alike, in which criteria for the good life are invested less in possession, surfaces and speed and more in appreciation, substance and a sense of the mystery at the heart of life. To be human in Jesus's way is *to walk humbly with God.*

Kathy Galloway

And what does the Lord require of you
but to do justice,
and to love kindness,
and to walk humbly with your God?

Micah 6:8 (NRSV)

November 4

TRAVELLING

I remember a story of European travellers of the last century pushing the pace through the African bush and their bearers eventually refusing to go any further. They said they must wait for their souls to catch up.

Travelling slowly our senses can pick up a lot more: the feel of the wind on the face, the sound of traffic and birdsong, the slope of the ground, the smells, the colours, the shape of the distant horizon. Much of this might be taken in unconsciously, but the final effect could still be a strong sense of connection between where one had started the journey and the place one arrived.

David Osborne, a member of the Iona Community, in an article about a pilgrimage to Iona

The wind blows where it wills,
and you hear the sound of it,
but you do not know whence it comes or whither it goes;
so it is with everyone who is born of Spirit.

John 3:8

November 5

JOURNEY BLESSING

May our journey ahead
be blessed with
God's laughter,
silences,
risks,
challenges,
healings,
questions,
promises,
protests,
answers,
tears,
solidarity,
often uncomfortable peace and
compassion-filled surprises –
perhaps all in one day.

Peter Millar

THE PERSONAL IS ALWAYS POLITICAL

The more personal we are, the more we have to confront the needs and claims of the community … To love a person is also to be concerned about the community in which he or she must live. To neglect one is to neglect the other. The personal is always political – but the political only becomes real, not theoretical, when it is grounded in the personal.

Kathy Galloway

COMMUNICATING HOPE

Jesus said: 'As the Father sent me so I send you, and before you go receive the Holy Spirit.'

Regularly in the New Testament, Spirit and hope go together. We heard in Paul: 'May God enlighten the eyes of your mind so that you can see what hope his call holds for you.'

We are called to communicate hope.

The twenty-first century has come to birth in a time of deep insecurity. What a nonsense seem the heady days of millennial optimism just a couple of years ago. The disorder of a Good Friday century has corrupted the beginnings of the young new century.

The pastoral and missionary task of authentic Christian living is clear. The call of Christ and the anxiety of the world say to us: communicate hope.

What does it mean to communicate hope?

Here's an answer:

- It's a disposition that cherishes all signs of new life, ready every moment to help to birth that which is ready to be born and does not become desperate or frantic when neither seems to be happening.

- Here's another: When the forms of an old way of being church are dying the new emerges when a few people are not afraid to be insecure.

- And another: Let us learn to give good burials to old ideas and ways and not keep digging them up to see if they've any life left.

- And another: Let each church give room to its dreamers and innovators to research possibilities, and not freeze them out through lack of trust and unwillingness to accept the pain of moving from death to life.

- And another: Hope in Christ produces a robust character in us that is not frightened of struggle, does not fear failure, and does not believe that the scars caused by Good Friday vulnerability are an embarrassment.

To communicate hope is not the same as having a plan or having a brighter idea than anyone else. To communicate hope is not the same as sounding convincing ...

John Rackley, a member of the Iona Community

November 8

Think it possible that you may be mistaken

From Quaker Advices and Queries 17

November 9
International Day Against
Fascism & Anti-Semitism

Resistance to oppression cannot begin too soon. There must be a refusal to accept or condone humiliation or any denial of human rights at its very first appearance. Elias Chacour, a Palestinian writer, once said, 'The holocaust began when the first person was able to say 'dirty Jew' and get away with it.'

Helen Steven, a member of the Iona Community

November 10

I am a soldier of Christ. I cannot fight.

St Martin of Tours (316–397)

November 11

We have no obligation to succeed. We do have an obligation to have a damn good try.

George MacLeod

November 12

I am slowly making my way through the crowds in a local store. Across the racks of clothing an old Muslim with a white beard is waving to me. At last we meet. I have known him for years. He served for well over 20 years in what he always called the 'British' army. He is still tall, slim and as straight as a ramrod. We exchange Christmas greetings and he goes on his way.

Soon after the beginning of the Second World War his regiment was sent from India to North Africa. When North Africa fell to the German and Italian forces he was taken prisoner. All the prisoners were sent to Italy but during the voyage his ship was torpedoed by a British submarine. He was rescued from the sea by the Italian navy and spent the rest of the war in a prison camp in Italy.

Stanley Hope, a member of the Iona Community

November 13

Each person is a chance for humanity.

Father Joseph Wresinski (1917–1988), founder of ATD Fourth World

SIN

The essence of sin is 'other people telling me who I am and I believing them'. Collusion with inauthentic images of myself can only be a denial of the irreducible originality of the given self, and thus an offence to God. In this sense sin is linked to a great deal of ill-health; for to believe and enact a lie about myself, however unconsciously or for whatever noble motives, can only be conducive to sickness.

From *Mud and Stars: a report on the impact of hospice experience on the Church's ministry of healing*

MUCH TO ANSWER FOR

Perhaps some of this arrogance stems from the very exclusivity of our own Christianity. If our belief is that the only way to salvation is through faith in Christ, and that all other faiths are lost to perdition, then the very seeds of dominance over all other religions are sown. We indeed have much to answer for in our destruction of other cultures and beliefs through our invasive evangelisation.

Helen Steven

November 16

Is there any way in which the poor of your own town or city could know, through the life of your own congregation, that God has seen their distress? Has such a message as that been delivered by your congregation with such substantial reality that the afflicted bow down and worship? Or, have you, rather, given them the impression that what God desires for them is that they should attend church services, dress neatly, listen to sermons, and put money in the plate for the upkeep of the building?

Reverend John Miller, former Moderator of the Church of Scotland, and minister of Castlemilk East

November 17

If the only prayer you ever said was, 'Thank you,'
that would be enough.

Meister Eckhart, 14th-century Christian mystic

November 18

IF THE POPE FLEW A KITE

I spent a wonderful day in the House of Hospitality, a centre for homeless street people in São Paulo, Brazil. There a banner hangs above the entrance of an empty tomb, and the empathic words 'Christo Vive!' (Christ Lives!). And certainly there were more signs of his resurrection presence in that community than in many a church I have visited.

Rubem Alves, one of the founding fathers of liberation theology, seemed to put his finger on something when he told me, 'I would believe more in the Church if the Pope flew a kite.' The Church, he feels, ought to be a place of laughter and celebration, of vision and dream. And yet the Church all too often behaves as if the burdens of the world are upon her shoulders.

Alves also said that he believed the real purpose of education ought to be to turn adults into children. Perhaps one of the most poignant moments of our whole three months in Brazil demonstrated that point. Robbie, our eldest son (who was three-and-a-half at the time) and myself went along to spend some time in a children's project. For two hours I sat inside finding out about the world through a translator, while Robbie played outside with about fifty children from the neighbouring favela. Watching him and the other children playing, I became so aware of all the barriers which we create as we grow up that children know nothing about, until we teach them. Returning to this country, I have realised the ever more pressing need to try to break down those barriers, and to learn from others, including our children.

Martin Johnstone, an associate member of the Iona Community

What the new creation story is telling us today is that we are surrounded by mystery … the true mystics I have known here have been people who never lost the sense of the child in wonder. The mystic, after all, is the divine child in us all wanting to play in the universe.

Matthew Fox

In 2004, six youth associates of the Iona Community went to Jerusalem and the West Bank to meet with young Palestinians and Israelis working for justice and peace. Here are two stories from that trip:

FIRAS AND ITAI

Firas is in his early 20s. He is studying medicine in East Jerusalem. The suburb where the university stands is the site of a wall being built by the Israeli government. The reason given for this wall is security, but it doesn't run along the border between Israel and the West Bank. Instead it cuts into the West Bank, separating farmers from their land and families from their relatives. Students like Firas have more stresses than just academic deadlines. Firas told us of an evening returning from a placement at a hospital in the West Bank. Coming to a checkpoint he was prevented from passing on the whim of a soldier. Turning back to the town he had just come from he found it under missile attack. His only option was to sleep by the side of the road. It is not only Firas's freedom of movement that has been curtailed on a soldier's whim. He told us of a time when he went to the Dome of The Rock mosque, but was told: 'No man under 30 to come in today.' 'So what did you do?' we asked him. 'We prayed in the street.'

Itai is a few years older than Firas. He is also at university, studying physics. As an Israeli he was conscripted into the army at the age of 18, but now he is a member of 'Yesh Gvul' (meaning 'Enough!'), a group made up of people who refuse to serve in the army because, instead of being used for defence, it's being used as an occupying army. So what changed? we asked him. Itai says that young conscripts are brainwashed into thinking all Palestinians you meet are terrorists. He calls the Israeli occupation of Gaza and the West Bank 'criminal', but says that most Israelis don't know what's going on there and don't want to know. For refusing to do reservist duties Itai has been to jail twice. 'It's only a month. It's not so bad,' he told us. 'I can do some reading, get rid of my beer belly. But if you refuse at the age of 18 you're jailed for a year or more.'

Abi Sampson, a youth associate of the Iona Community

ISAIAH'S DREAM ON POLZEATH BEACH
Isaiah 2:4

We watched her from our car, parked on the sand, as she skipped along in her pink plastic wellies. She must have been all of three-and-a-half, and she carried a large plastic sword. Her little brother had a spade. It didn't matter – any stick would have been all right to poke in all the puddles and prod the sand.

It didn't enter her head to use the sword as a weapon, to cross sword and spade with her brother. No – she was tracing long furrows in the sand. She had innocently turned her sword into a ploughshare. Will we adults learn to follow the teachings of little children?

David Hawkey, an associate member of the Iona Community and former member of the resident group on Iona

The children are our most endangered species.

Daniel Berrigan

SEEKING PEACE

For nearly two decades I've been leading quiet days and retreats. It is great to see people turning to God, finding comfort and confidence for the struggles of daily experience there. It is exciting to see how prayer life is opened as it is explored in the context of stillness and silence. It is good that the spiritual journey is one that we can share with those beyond the church.

But we cannot afford the luxury of so focusing on the search for an inner peace that we neglect the search for world peace, justice for the peoples and cultures of our planet and reconciliation between religious communities ...

John Rackley, a member of the Iona Community

MUSIC TO MY EARS

I was neurotic for years. Anxious, depressed, selfish. And everyone kept telling me to change. And I resented them, and agreed with them, and wanted to change, but simply couldn't, no matter how hard I tried. I felt powerless and trapped. One day, God said: 'Don't change. I love you as you are.' These words were music to my ears. I relaxed. I came alive. And suddenly I changed.

Anthony de Mello

MISSION

A world where we look for and find the Spirit at work outside the present boundaries of the church.

A world where there is a genuine pluralism and where we respect, appreciate and learn from the religious beliefs of others.

A world where the Christian message is no longer identified with Western civilisation, and where we see many ways in which non-Christian cultures may be far closer than our own to the Christian vision and values.

A world where we have an integrated concept of human liberation and development, replacing the sharp dualisms of body and spirit, of this life and the next life, of church and the world, of nature and grace.

A world where patriarchal values and models of thought and action are being questioned and where we are called to give the feminine its full value …

Mission is not just a matter of doing things for people. It is first of all a matter of being with people, of listening and sharing with them.

Donal Dorr

Mission is being with Christ where the pain is.

John V. Taylor

November 24

Is it not the essence of prayer – to see the One who is always near, and who is constantly inviting us, in gentle compassion, to come back to our inheritance as a human being made in the divine image?

Peter Millar

November 25
International Day for the Elimination of Violence Against Women

A PEBBLE IN A POOL

This pebble produced ripples, sparkling ripples of hope in a pool of despond. A woman decided to walk the pebble-strewn path of the West Highland Way. She was sponsored to the tune of £1000. She had read an article in *Life and Work* magazine entitled 'Invisible Women', on the subject of trafficking in women, which had moved her. So she got in touch, and now the Forum has the responsibility of dispensing this gift. That pebble is now sending ripples through Europe. The pool is deep and dark, but the ripples will spread and bring hope to a few. Some of the gift will go to NGOs working with the traumatised survivors of trafficking in women in Eastern Europe, some to CHASTE, an interdenominational and independent charity here in the UK helping victims of trafficking, and some to educational work in Romania to prevent this harrowing trade.

Sally Beaumont, a member of the Iona Community

For the Christian, the seeming distresses of the days in which we live should not be cause for pessimism; they are rather the loud overture of some new and wondrous Revelation …

We believe not that God is trying to say something to us all above the storms of our present distress, rather that it is the storm that is His voice.

George MacLeod, 1938

God is not nice.
God is not an uncle.
God is an earthquake.

Hasidic saying

God is not an imperial controller and triumphant manager. He is a persevering artist, a suffering servant and an indefatigable and invincible lover.

David Jenkins

THE UNIQUE VALUE OF EVERY INDIVIDUAL

I am convinced that self-respect and an acknowledgement of the unique value of every individual is the essence of the gospel. Two years ago I was serving a short time in prison and was attempting to write a piece on the 'Good news to the poor' passage from Luke's gospel. I was trying to imagine coming out of my cell and telling fellow-prisoners that I had good news for them, and what it might be. Apart from telling them that they could all go free, I was stuck for ideas. It was a woman prisoner who gave me the answer. She was an alcoholic, and when I asked if she had ever thought of joining Alcoholics Anonymous, she pointed out that you have to want to stop drinking. When I asked why she didn't want to stop she said: 'Well, you see, you have to have some self-respect for that. I don't respect myself, and nobody else does.' It's not enough to tell her she's valuable to God – we have to accord her that degree of value in the way in which we treat her …

Helen Steven, a member of the Iona Community

STONES

The conversation with Naim Ateek came at the end of two exhausting weeks in Israel and Palestine. We had seen stones upon stones, and stones torn from stones. We had prayed at Masada as the sun rose. We had seen Palestinian olive trees torn from the land by bulldozers, and newly replanted mature olive trees on Israeli property, mysteriously supplied by Israeli contractors. We had been to a hospital to visit victims of the November 21st Jerusalem bus bombing. ('Thank you for coming to see us: we feel so alone.') We met an elderly Palestinian woman at 6:30 am in the Old City. She had left home in Bethlehem at 2 am, passed through umpteen aggressive checkpoints, and looked to sell a couple of bags of herbs. ('I struggle. Tell Bush and Sharon. It is their doing.') We attended Jewish Sabbath worship in a suburban gym hall, and timeless Armenian worship in their cathedral and at the Church of the Resurrection. We listened to a senior Israeli official who lives in a West Bank settlement telling us that 'the world must realise the unacceptability of the terror we endure on our land'. We had been shown by Israeli Arabs the detailed map of settlement encroachment on the West Bank, and been told by Israeli peace activists of their daily work in trying to limit the humiliation visited on Palestinians at checkpoints. At 2 am, we had seen the scrum of East Jerusalem Arabs desperately trying to ensure access to the Ministry office where, when the door opened at 8 am, a handful of them might get permission to stay in their own city.

And we saw more stones. The stones where Jesus had trod.

By the time we met Naim at his Sabeel Foundation office (Sabeel Ecumenical Liberation Theology Centre), our hearts were bursting, our senses reeling, our minds full. 'What can we as foreigners do to help you?'

'Tell the world that Palestine exists. Palestinians are now collectively suicidal. We despair. We want intervention.'

Danus Skene, a member of the Iona Community who spent 1998–99 as acting head teacher of Tabeetha School, the Church of Scotland's multicultural and multifaith school in Jaffa.

KEEPING HOPE ALIVE

The steadfast olive tree,
at home on the hillside,
at the door of the house,
is a silent witness.

Gnarled trunk, knuckled limbs
telling the tale of years,
grey-green leaves quivering like laughter –
leaves shaped like tears.

Frugal, it flourishes in poor soil;
generous, it nourishes the people:
bearing fruit in season,
yielding healing oil.

Its roots hold together dry earth,
branches give shelter from the sun:
it clothes the land;
it is rooted in the land.

It is a promise of peace.

Needed and taken for granted,
it stands for the future of the people.

What is left when it is gone?

Now, when homes are destroyed
and a way of life swept away,
the olive trees are uprooted,
hillsides are bare – what is left?

A fragile sapling planted
close against the fence
that divides the land
and threatens mortal danger:

an olive tree taking root
grey-green leaves flickering in the wind,
under the sun, a silent witness;
maybe

a sign of hope.

Jan Sutch Pickard, written during a visit to the Holy Land

November 30

CHOOSE LIFE

I listened to Prof. James Whyte of St Andrews recalling Dennis Potter's television play *Son of Man*.

'There was one scene,' he said, 'that had no basis in the Gospels, a piece of pure imagination. There was a scene where Jesus and his disciples chance on a place of execution where some criminals, or some rebels, have been crucified.

'The Roman soldiers are taking bodies down from the cross. The crowds slowly disperse, but the disciples linger at the scene of horror, beside the empty crosses.

'Jesus, in anguish of emotion at the callousness and the cruelty of men, puts his arms round the cross and hides his face against it.

'Then the carpenter in him takes over, and his hands are telling him something as he feels the wood under his expert fingertips, and he stands back in surprise.

'"This is good timber. Look at that. Straight from the heart of the tree. Not a knot in it … you could split that straight … make tables and chairs … we can make tables, chairs, good things, useful things. But what do men make? A cross!"'

'That scene,' said Prof. Whyte, 'that piece of pure imagining, has stuck in my mind since I first saw it. The Carpenter of Nazareth, admiring the timber of which a cross was made, and wondering in horror that men, given such good material, make from it – a cross!

'Look at the world today – at what you read in the newspapers or see on the television news – and ask why it is that the human race, given so many blessings, turn them into curses?

'Given the choice of life and good, we choose instead death and evil! Why, from the wonderful timber of a tree, make the ugly torture of a cross? Why do nations with hungry mouths to feed and families poorly housed choose instead the weapons of mass destruction?'

Recalling the words of the writer of Deuteronomy, Prof. Whyte concluded, 'See, I have set before you this day life and death, blessing and curse. Therefore choose life.'

Professor James Whyte, as told by Erik Cramb

December

LETTERS FROM GUGULETU

In 2005, the Iona Community received an invitation from Reverend Dr Spiwo Xapile, minister at J.L. Zwane Memorial Presbyterian Church in Guguletu, a black township of 250,000 people near Cape Town, for someone from the Iona Community to walk alongside the folk in Guguletu and reflect with them on their work. Peter Millar and Nick Prance, at different times, both took up this invitation. Here are two excerpts from their letters to the Iona Community from Guguletu.

Isaac's story: The most marvellous music

… But I want to mention something positive and encouraging also, something about what is possible, something transforming, and that is Isaac's story.

Isaac is 18 years old and has spent all his life in Guguletu. He has never known his father, then several years ago his mother died of AIDS. Isaac now lives with relatives who have been offering much care and support. I just want to pause here to acknowledge the remarkable level of costly family support that goes on in these communities. There are huge numbers of grandmothers in particular, but also aunts and various other members of extended family, looking after orphaned children in often the most demanding of situations, and in doing so they are quietly helping to give people like Isaac at least something of a chance. Isaac also regularly goes to the J.L. Zwane Centre, where there is an after school programme, assistance with homework, the provision of a meal, and sometimes food parcels. In addition to this, the centre also hosts social activities, and through this Isaac has learned to play the marimba. To be honest 'learned to play' doesn't do him justice. The other night I was sitting in my room adjacent to the centre, when I heard the most marvellous music coming from around the corner. It was infectious in its energy and rhythm and, after about ten minutes, I couldn't sit with my book any longer – I had to find the source of this sound that just made me want to move my feet! So I explored; and just outside an adjacent garage I found several of the young people, including Isaac, making rhythms that would grace any stage. And there was dancing too, the girls working out routines to the infectious sound.

Life for Isaac is still not easy, and when we talked recently he was **uncertain** about his future and what it might hold. But he feels he has one, and is optimistic, and we have talked about the possibility of his volunteering on Iona. Much of this hope is down to an awful lot of caring by a lot of people – and Isaac's strength of character. Carers and centres like J.L. Zwane need and deserve all the support they can get, because they are making such a difference in people's lives.

Whilst talking about the plight of orphans, it is worth drawing **attention to the** fact that yesterday (Tuesday 25 October, 2005) Kofi Annan helped to launch the United Nations Children's Fund five-year HIV/AIDS awareness programme, 'Unite for children, unite against AIDS', to highlight the plight of the millions of children infected, or affected, by this disease that has deprived 15 million children of one or both parents. The campaign also reminds us that 1,400 children under the age of 15 die every day from AIDS or a related illness. If you want to know more about this campaign you can find details at www.unicef.org/uniteforchildren/

To conclude, yesterday I attended the HIV/AIDS support group again; it was a mixed bag. First there was a presentation from an insurance company representative selling group funeral plans. It was pretty sombre. And then one of the leaders took over. Once again I didn't understand much of what was going on as it was in Xhosa, but at one point the leader got VERY animated. I mean, I was sitting next to her and could have done with earplugs. And the word 'condom' made an appearance, no, several appearances, and then this woman was virtually off her seat making very suggestive thrusting gestures and little noises, and everyone in the room was howling with laughter and slapping their thighs, using their whole body to laugh … It was impossible not to laugh along, just at the level of mirth in the room and my interpretation of what she was getting at; and then she changed tack and said something about AIDS – and you could have heard a pin drop. I think she got her message across. Such life and death once more inhabiting the same space.

Nick Prance

Incredible risks

In a couple of hours many hundreds of people will be here at the church to watch an amazing musical performed by the equally amazing music group, which is part of the ministry. It is about HIV/AIDS, and holds the audience absolutely spellbound for an hour and a half. Earlier today, as they do each week, several hundred high school children from many areas of Cape Town came to watch the musical. I don't think I exaggerate when I say that this musical must be one of the best AIDS-awareness programmes in Africa, and it is tremendous that the group is able to take it to many venues far beyond Guguletu.

And this brings me back to the question of how people in other places, far from South Africa, can help. It will be an issue that we shall be discussing within the Iona Community after my return at the end of May.

One answer is this: Do everything in your power to place global poverty at the heart of your government's agenda. The present global economic structures are – as we all know – wounding millions of our sisters and brothers, a truth which jumps out at me every day in Guguletu where HIV/AIDS can never be seen in isolation from the prevailing, and I believe increasing, poverty.

It is a heart-breaking situation in many ways, but when I witness the incredible risks for love which people are taking here in the fight against unemployment, lack of housing, and HIV/AIDS (to name but a few of the realities here), I believe with Desmond Tutu (whose home is just a few miles down the road) that a day will come when poverty will no longer imprison his sisters and brothers, and a brighter Light will shine on his special land. Only then will freedom truly come to South Africa.

Peter Millar

Prayer

Watch now, dear Lord,
with those who wake or watch or weep tonight,
and give your angels charge over those who sleep.
Tend your sick ones, O Lord Christ,
rest your weary ones,
bless your dying ones, soothe your suffering ones,
pity your afflicted ones, shield your joyous ones,
and all for your love's sake. Amen.

And now may the God of hope
fill us with all joy and peace in believing,
that we may abound in hope
in the power of the Holy Spirit. Amen

St Augustine, from *Iona Abbey Worship Book*

December 2
United Nations International
Day for the Abolition of Slavery

On the coast of Ghana sit two 'castles', prisons for many millions of Africans who were captured into slavery in past centuries – 15 million transported to the Americas. It was on this trade in humans as commodities that wealth in Europe was built. Over the cells, where the slaves were imprisoned waiting for deportation, was a chapel. Christians worshipped God while directly below, right under their feet, those being sold into slavery languished in chains.

Adapted from a message to the Churches, World Alliance of Reformed Churches Council, Accra 2004

December 3

The flickering light of Advent is a faint and vulnerable thing, but somehow refuses to allow the overwhelming blackness to snuff it out totally.

Ron Ferguson

Carrying a candle
from one little place of shelter
to another
is an act of love.

To move through the huge
and hungry darkness, step by step,

against the invisible wind
that blows for ever around the world,
carrying a candle,
is an act of foolhardy hope.

Surely it will be blown out:
the wind is contemptuous,
the darkness cannot comprehend it.
How much light can this tiny flame shed
on all the great issues of the day?
It is as helpless as a newborn child.

Look how the human hand,
that cradles it, has become translucent:
fragile and beautiful; foolish and loving.
Step by step.

The wind is stronger than this hand,
and the darkness infinite
around this tiny here-and-now flame,
that wavers, but keeps burning:
carried with such care
through an uncaring world
from one little place of shelter to another.
An act of love.

The light shines in the darkness
and the darkness can never put it out.

Jan Sutch Pickard, a member of the Iona Community

December 4

We have all known the long loneliness and we have learned the only solution is love and that love comes from community.

Dorothy Day

December 5

I believe that knowledge of death among the populace has multiplied tenfold in recent years; it can simply no longer be overlooked. What, though, are we doing with our knowledge of death, with our experience of impotence, with our cowardice? We sit there like paralysed rabbits facing the snake. This paralysis, this fear, this consciousness of impotence is the spiritual problem of our time. We simply do not believe Christ, who said to the despairing disciples: 'Everything is possible to those who believe.'

Dorothee Soelle

December 6

LISTENING

How can the birth and life of Jesus root us in the lifelong struggle to stand with the marginalised, in Afghanistan, in AIDS/HIV wards, in refugee camps, in the affluent West? What will it take to make us, individually and corporately, stop, reflect, pause – wait – before delivering our response to terror in either word or war?

Years ago I read a compelling Quaker pamphlet called 'Creative Listening' by Rachel Pinney. In it she describes how the seemingly simple act of listening can be terribly difficult to practise. So often we hear the words of others while formulating our own thoughts for a response. She writes of the need to listen with an empty mind and to pause before responding, to allow the words of the other to inform (and reform) our own thoughts. If applied to personal relationships this can be transforming. If adopted by governments and world leaders this could be revolutionary ... It is in the waiting and the stillness that the impetus to act creatively is given the space to be born.

Ruth Harvey, a member of the Iona Community

The first duty of love is to listen.

Paul Tillich

December 7

SEEKING GOD IN 'THE OTHER'

Ideological and psychological control of people's minds and opinions is another of the building blocks of oppression, often whipped up and exaggerated by a controlled media. The speed with which exaggerated enemy images and demonisation can occur is particularly alarming. Against a background of 'Saddam the Rat', 'Hang Saddam Long and Slow' I had the temerity to suggest to the Military staff College at Camberley that we should attempt to listen to the Iraqi side of the story. My audience actually hissed! There is such a huge task of listening and creating safe spaces where such listening can happen. There is a delicate balance between retelling history to enable better understanding and dwelling on past bitterness to foster hatred. But only when history is listened to, grievances acknowledged, and past hurts shared, can memory become a healing and reconciling process. There is much we can do to encourage real healing.

There are many examples of creative work which challenge our stereotypes. During the Cold War a huge poster which bore the slogan 'The Russians Are Coming' showed a beautiful picture of a Bolshoi ballerina. At the end of the Gulf War a week was held in the Abbey on Iona for Jews, Christians and Muslims to share their experiences of living in Britain during the war. Recently a small group came together in the Nonviolence Centre in Dunblane simply to share their confusion and bewilderment about the war in Kosovo, and at the end of October a delegation is going from Scotland to Bosnia to visit joint Christian-Muslim reconciliation projects in Sarajevo and Tuzla. It requires a constant seeking for 'that of God' in the other and (no matter how hard it seems) a refusal ever to let other human beings be demeaned or humiliated.

Helen Steven, a member of the Iona Community

December 8

THE FUTURE

What is our vision for the future of multiracial Britain? Do we want a society where there is racial segregation and racial inequality, or a society where there is equal respect and racial equality? As an old Pakistani said recently on the radio, 'For years we have lived side by side. We must now learn to live together.'

Stanley Hope, a member of the Iona Community

RESIST TRIDENT – CELEBRATE HOPE

So I am telling you:
If you are not saying no,
you're saying yes.
Silence is consent,
silence is complicity.
Stand up and be counted.
Don't spectate – participate.
Don't be paralysed by analysis.
Walk the talk.
If not you – who?
And if not now – when?
Get active – not radioactive.
Don't spectate – demonstrate.
Don't sit on the fence – cut it
like all those women did
at Greenham Common.
Remember Rosa Parks.
Get your butt to the front,
and the front is Faslane.
Experience empowerment.
Live liberation through participation.

Resist Trident – Celebrate hope

Brian Quail, a member of the Iona Community, from 'Resistance and Hope Rap'

Make us keep the spluttering lantern burning
and not break a wounded reed
Make us understand
the secret of eternal life
from the pulse of blood in our veins
and realise the worth of a life
from the movement of a warm heart
Make us not discriminate
the rich from the poor
the high from the low
the learned from the ignorant
those we know well and those we
do not know
    Oh!
A human life can't be exchanged for the whole world
This supreme task of keeping the lives
of the sons and daughters of God.
Let us realise how lovely it is
to feel the burdens of responsibility

By a worker of the Peace Market, Korea

ONE OLD WOMAN (SUNDAY MORNING IN WARSAW)

… My fellow worshippers were crouched under their hands, mostly women, mostly on their own. Their posture was one of grovelling sorrow. At the passing of the peace only people who knew each other exchanged perfunctory handshakes. No one else moved. I left before the sermon droned to a halt.

Outside in relief, breathing the lively cold air, watching the golden leaves catch the morning sun, I realised I had missed the offertory. There was one other person on my side of the street. She was literally bent double – more than double, since her rump was higher than her head. A grey grubby skeletal hand, trembling like a leaf, appeared from a dusty shawl; and I heard a high tiny voice from under the same shawl. Then I saw her whole body was shivering violently.

So that is where my offertory money went – into that freezing hand. I never even saw her face; but clearly she was surprised and pleased with the 20 zloti note (about 4 pounds), rather than the coppers she expected.

Then I found myself angry – once again. It was simply not OK by me that the education and intelligence of those highly paid men who run the world financial system, combined with the staggering inventiveness of our runaway technology, should produce – instead of plenty for everyone – an economic system in which even *one* old woman in any country should have to freeze in the street as she begs for bread while others make fortunes doing nothing more or less useful than buying and selling money.

And it is not just one. Every year there are more and more. Old people and young people and children … And there are alternatives; and these men who run the world know there are. We live in a world of plenty, and they treat the rest of us as though it were a world of scarcity. The problem is not production, the problem is distribution. But they make light of the suffering of poor people, and they make heavy weather of the difficulties of introducing alternatives.

Margaret Legum, a member of the Iona Community

December 12

If we have Bibles and communion, why do we need doctrine conceived in another's civilisation? Why should we need Augustine, Aquinas, Barth and Tillich, when in our own past we have Beyanawidah, Tecumseh, Quetzalcoatl and Chilan Balan?

From a letter by a Native American to Ian M Fraser

Listen and learn, and then listen to us more.

An Aboriginal leader

December 13

People travel great distances to find holiness. Some even come to Iona.

There is the story of a boy who lived in an isolated house on a hill. A God-forsaken place for a young man. But one thing fascinated him. Each night he would look out into the darkness and see a light. It was far away on a hilltop, but this sign of life gave him hope.

One day he decided to go in search of it. It was a long and lonely walk, and it was already dark before he reached the outskirts of a town. Tired and hungry, he knocked at the first door he came to, and explained his search for the mysterious light that had always given him hope.

'I know it!' replied the woman who had answered the door. 'It gives me hope as well.' And she pointed back in the direction from which he had come. There, on the horizon, was a single light shining. A sign of life in the darkness. The light from his house.

Brian Woodcock , a member of the Iona Community and former warden of Iona Abbey

December 14

In the first place it should be known that if anyone is seeking God, the Beloved is seeking that person much more.

St John of the Cross (1542–1591)

For every step we take towards God, he takes a thousand steps towards us.

Paraphrased from the Koran

December 15

A candle-light is a protest at midnight.
It is a non-conformist.
It says to the darkness,
'I beg to differ.'

Fr Samuel Rayan, Christian conference of Asia, Singapore, 1984

THE GIFT OF MAKING FRIENDS

One Sunday afternoon before Christmas I went to see a Muslim widow who had just returned from Bangladesh. Her husband had died in the late summer and she had flown to Bangladesh with his body for burial. He had died one evening. That morning a phone call from Bangladesh had told her that her sister had died. For her it was a double tragedy. She told me: 'They are buried side by side and next to my father. As a widow I cannot live in Bangladesh. My home is here now, in England.'

It was a loss for me too. I had known her husband for over 30 years, before they were married. He came here intending to be a barrister but it never happened and he worked for years in a local factory until he became ill and died. He was a remarkable man, quiet, never self-important, always calm. He had a tremendous knowledge of world history, politics, colonialism and religion. From him, in many visits to their home, I learned so much.

His wife came here at the age of 18, a woman with a wonderful smile, which she never lost, but not speaking a word of English. Her way of learning English was to start work in a sewing factory alongside white women. Consequently, she does not speak textbook English, but like a native. They had one child, a girl, who recently qualified as a doctor and will work in this country.

As we sat together she spoke of her marriage. 'He was a good man, always kind to me. We were married for 28 years. He gave me so much freedom. I drove a car. I could go wherever I wanted. I made several English friends. I went to parties in the factory and was always accepted and respected. At home we seldom had an argument.' She has the gift of making friends across barriers of race and culture.

Stanley Hope, a member of the Iona Community

Faith is entrusting ourselves to this mystery in which we are living, trusting that love is at the heart of it, so that it is safe to explore, unsafe to rest in what we consider our present certainties ... Nothing so masks the face of God as our own certainties. With faith in God we see everything as provisional, and we are always open to new possibilities.

Gerard Hughes

NOW

The word 'Now' occurs often in the New Testament, especially in reference to the coming of the day of the Lord.

We are all too apt to think of religion in terms of the past or of the future. God, we think, was active in the past. God, we hope, will be active in the future. The present is the interval in which we are left alone, to enjoy or to endure, but nothing of importance is likely to happen now.

But the only way we can speak of God is in the present: God is. The only time when we can know God is now. The only time we can serve him is now.

Now is the time of the Lord's coming. Now is the only time that matters to us. Now is the only door to the future.

Ralph Morton, a founding member of the Iona Community

December 19

Just to be is a blessing. Just to live is holy.

Abraham Joshua Heschel

December 20

THICK PLACES

George MacLeod is often quoted as saying Iona is a thin place – with small boundaries between material and spiritual. Only the thickness of a tissue between heaven and earth. I love this and I experience it here. This seems to me to be a place 'shot through with the Glory of God'. It's so important to have this experience precisely because it helps us, it nurtures us, when we're in the THICK places – the God-forsaken places, the ugly places – places of death and oppression where Jesus's presence can hardly be felt or experienced with any spontaneity.

These are places where Christ comes to us in the guise of a stranger – in the hookers, crooks, and thieves just like the crowd Jesus made his best friends and in whom he promises to hide himself.

Is not our spiritual pilgrimage a daily journey of taking up the cross to see the presence of God – to see the executed and risen Christ in the most unlovely places so that we can be led to resist and struggle and advocate and agitate and present our bodies as living sacrifices against all that hurts and maims and insults and kills God's children? This is not an easy pilgrimage because it inevitably brings conflict with the powerful and 'the money boys', as George MacLeod loved to call them. Struggling for the poor and exploited means pushing with all our strength against the powerful tides of global capitalism and its maniacal, frenetic demands to buy more, consume more, trample our neighbours, and ignore the common good in our desperate pursuit of our own personal comfort, titillation, pleasure and convenience. And this struggle is never welcomed by the powers.

Murphy Davis, The Open Door Community, Atlanta, Georgia

December 21

BREAD

The cost of Trident is equivalent to spending £30,000 a day since the birth of Christ. Is this what we, as a so-called society, really consider to be a responsible use of our money? I work in partnership with families living in poverty and social exclusion in Glasgow. I would be failing these people, whom I feel privileged to call my friends, if I did not make a stand against this obscene expenditure.

Molly Harvey, a member of the Iona Community

Jim Garrison, an American theologian, once told this story:

A monk had a dream. He was walking down a street when an aeroplane flew overhead and dropped a bomb. Instinctively everyone knew it was a nuclear weapon, and all scattered – except the monk. He felt he must catch the bomb before it exploded and destroyed everyone. He caught it, and the bomb turned to bread in his hands. He broke the bread and shared it, seeking out those who had run away and drawing them back into community.

Joy Mead, a member of the Iona Community

December 22

HOPE

One of the most important distinctions I have learned in the course of reflection on Jewish history is the difference between 'optimism' and 'hope'. Optimism is the belief that things will get better. Hope is the faith that, together, we can make things better. Optimism is a passive virtue, hope an active one. It takes no courage to be an optimist, but it takes a great deal of courage to have hope. Knowing what we do of our past, no Jew can be an optimist. But Jews have never – despite a history of sometimes awesome suffering – given up hope. Not by accident did they call the national anthem of their new state 'Hatvikvah', meaning, 'the hope'.

Chief Rabbi Jonathan Saks

December 23

NIGHT BLESSING

May you be out of your depth –
as the deeps of the night sky
contain but cannot explain God's mystery.
May you lose count –

as an infinity of stars
is dazed and amazed by God's presence.
May you be in the dark –
as the moon is eclipsed, but held safe,
with all that is, in the palm of God's hand.
May you be lost for words –
as the Word is spoken
in the silence of the night,
in the beauty of God's creation.

Jan Sutch Pickard, a member of the Iona Community

A STORY OF HOPE

On Christmas Eve 1993 I was in Nazareth. The town was packed with people from all over the country for the Christmas parade, perhaps for a moment resembling the chaos of the first Christmas in a town a few hours drive south.

At the head of the parade, in the Nazareth tradition, were the leaders of all the Christian traditions, along with the local Muslim cleric and the Communist mayor. They all went to school together and so find walking together more straightforward than others in similar roles in other places.

Suddenly, I thought I could hear a familiar sound – bagpipes. I was hallucinating, homesick maybe. But no. It grew louder and suddenly there they were – Muslim scouts dressed in tartan sashes playing 'White Christmas' on Jordanian bagpipes!

That's interfaith for you.

Ewan Aitken, a member of the Iona Community

CHRIST, BE OUR LIGHT

Longing for light, we wait in darkness.
Longing for truth, we turn to you.
Make us your own, your holy people,
light for the world to see.
>   *Christ, be our light!*
>   *Shine in our hearts,*
>   *Shine through the darkness.*
>   *Christ, be our light!*
>   *Shine in your church*
>   *gathered today.*

Longing for peace, our world is troubled.
Longing for hope, many despair.
Your word alone has power to save us.
Make us your living voice.
>   *Chorus*

Longing for food, many are hungry.
Longing for water, many still thirst.
Make us your bread, broken for others,
shared until all are fed.
>   *Chorus*

Longing for shelter, many are homeless.
Longing for warmth, many are cold.
Make us your building, sheltering others,
walls made of living stone.
>   *Chorus*

Many the gifts, many the people,
many the hearts that yearn to belong.
Let us be servants to one another,
making your kingdom come.
Chorus

Bernadette Farrell
A song often sung in Iona Abbey

GLORY TO GOD IN THE HIGH ST

A boy threw a stone at a stained-glass window of the incarnation. It nicked out the 'E' in the word HIGHEST in the text GLORY TO GOD IN THE HIGH-EST. Thus, till it was unfortunately mended, it read, GLORY TO GOD IN THE HIGH ST.

At least the mended E might have been contrived on a swivel so that in a high wind it would have been impossible to see which way it read.

Such is the genius, and the offence, of the Christian revelation.

Holiness, salvation, glory are all come down to earth in Jesus Christ our Lord …

George MacLeod

CHRISTMAS REFLECTION

Four Christmas dawns have come
since 'the war on terror' was birthed
in the heart of global wealth
and we moved into a new fragility –
that unknown place, bereft of joy,
now defining our times,
with its markers of
alienation and fear.
A place where the stranger
is to be
passed by,
scrutinised,
driven from home,
imprisoned –
perhaps even tortured in the name of truth.
And yet, and yet,
despite it all,
still in our midst,
visionary spirits,
courageous prophets of our age,
tenderly remind us that,
strange as it may seem,
we are all made in the image
of the one God
whose justice
is so different from our own,
and whose unfathomable love still holds our humanity intact.

Peter Millar, Christmas 2005

For God's foolishness is wiser than human wisdom, and God's weakness is stronger than human strength.

1 Corinthians 1:25 (NRSV)

December 26

One survivor of the tsunami, Pat Faragher, returned shoeless from holiday in Sri Lanka. With her husband, Bill, at her side, she stood at Heathrow in her socks and said: 'We have lost everything – no passports, no papers, all our belongings were swept away. But we're alive.' Alive, with a sense of what really matters. A stripped-down, less-cluttered sense of human identity is what we need for citizenship in the wounded global village. It should go hand in hand with an abandonment of the illusory control of our world.

The Indian Ocean tragedy drives home the interconnectedness of our world. We are our brothers' and sisters' keepers, and they ours. We humans have the power to visit the sins of the fathers and mothers on future generations, and it is a terrible power. The tide-borne, hollow-eyed ghosts in our living rooms ask profound questions. And, in these questions, if we have ears to hear and eyes to see, we may even discern the voice of God.

Ron Ferguson

A DIFFERENT RANDOMNESS

The utterly random nature of so much of life is about the only certainty we have between birth and death. It is a futile debate to ask why life is random, for we can only be sure that it is. It is futile to speculate about what life would be were there no such things as earthquakes, tidal waves, droughts and other vagaries of the awesome power of nature. It's like trying to wonder what life would be like if there was a certain lifespan, say we all lived to 70 where none died young, or lived to be 100. All we can say is that it would not be life as we know it. Life as we know it has a random power beyond our controlling. There is also a different randomness of our human making which we call sin and which cumulatively, through the greed and wickedness of some, condemns others to a lifetime of unwarranted and unavoidable poverty and fragility…

Erik Cramb, a member of the Iona Community

AN IMPRESSION ON THE DARKNESS

The world is struggling to take in the scale of the disaster – shocked by the images of suffering and devastation we have seen on our TV screens. In the Sunday review programmes there was much asking of the questions, 'Where was God?', 'How could God allow this to happen?' and we are all challenged to look at what is fundamental in our faith. A panel of Hindu, Buddhist, Muslim and Christian representatives agreed that there may be no answer to 'why?', but what is important is how we respond. And that is always what matters – just one candle makes an impression on the darkness. We must keep lighting the ones within our reach, for, shocking as this has been, there are so many other candles which need lighting – and thank God so many of you light them in all sorts of different ways and places, keeping hope alive!

Lynda Wright, a member of the Iona Community, in a letter from Key House,
a Christian retreat centre in Falkland, Scotland

CALM BROWN EYES FIXED ON ME

We sat in a Muslim home: three women, two men, myself and three small children. We talked about a younger brother at present in Bangladesh with his mother looking for a suitable wife. A baby, perhaps six months old, was passed around as if it were the most natural thing in the world. When the child was passed to me I looked down into the calm brown eyes fixed on me. What did the future hold for this baby? In 20 years would the world be a more friendly place? And will there be in Britain a true multi-ethnic society where all are valued and accepted regardless of race or colour?

Stanley Hope, a member of the Iona Community

BLESSING

I heard this blessing in the Royston Rainbow Club. It was Christmas time and a homeless person was receiving a welcomed dinner. It was straight from the heart and has stayed with me for over 30 years.

'Ach, God bless yih, in the name of Mary, Joseph, and ra wee man.'

From Larry Nugent, a member of the Iona Community

Do not neglect to show hospitality to strangers, for by doing that some have entertained angels without knowing it.

Hebrews 13:2 (NRSV)

December 29

Follow the truth wherever you find it.
Even if it takes you outside your preconceived ideas of God or life.
Even if it takes you outside your own country
into the most insignificant alien places
like Bethlehem.
Be courageous. But concentrate on your search.
Truth is one. All roads lead to home.

George MacLeod

December 30

IONA MOMENTS

On Iona you become intensely aware of the moment. 'Iona is a place of moments,' Kathy Galloway once told me. A place of amazing sunsets, brilliant conversations, incredible meetings. A place where the mood of the weather can change by the minute; where you can experience sunshine, hail and rainbows all in a half-hour.

A place where storms blow over and joy comes out unexpectedly. Where tourists come for the day, guests stay a week, and residents and volunteers remain for a moment of their lives. A place where the ferry keeps coming and going across the stretch of time, bringing change, disturbing routine.

'So, why did you come to Iona?' visitors ask. And I think one answer is: to learn to live more fully in the moment.

Iona moments: pages from a diary (To Helen)
Luke 17:20–21

Little, Big moments:

Like stopping to notice the way light falls and rocks glow. Wonderful little, Big moments that make the heart dance again. Moments when I suddenly become aware of all the overwhelming beauty and wonder and richness and love living in the middle of where I'm standing already, and I gaze around understanding: the Kingdom of God is now.

✳

Moments with friends:

Alice, who used to sell antique jewellery, talking about a bonfire on the beach: how she stood and watched the waves steam and hiss; how she can see things here, *really* see things. How the other day the sea was like silver. And the crest of a wave – the very top that hung there – like a peridot she sold one time. How she's seeing things with a different value now. A new preciousness.

Julie sharing how one morning she ran up Dun I chasing after the sunrise – explaining she has migraines usually that keep her down. But that one clear morning woke up early and looked out, and ran up Dun I. Climbed thinking about how she could never find her niche in life, was always chasing after something, never catching up. And needed to reach the top before the sunrise, and arms outstretched made it, and cried and laughed. Then, thought about all the prisoners in the world who never even see the sun. Then, how we are all prisoners in ourselves. And prayed for all prisoners.

Lynne, beautiful Lynne, talking about playing her recorder in a communion service. And how in the perfect silence after the last whole note she felt some-one else there besides her. *Beside her.* About how God speaks in silences.

Moments listening to friends. The feeling in the moment after of something holy that hangs in the air. The resonance of something beyond words. Like the feeling you experience after hearing a beautiful poem, or song, or prayer; in the moment after the breaking of the bread with the wine held up.

Com-panion (to break bread with).

Moments in meetings:

The cook at All Staff who shared how she had lost her taste for life, and found its savour again here – can taste, smell, feel again. Thank you, Lord. How, in the end, she told us, it was she who was fed.

Someone else saying they feel at home: at home in themselves. And that they are learning to feel the grace through the sorrow. 'The deeper joy within.'

The warm smell of the kitchen reaching in as we share our stories: This life like the rich, healthy smell of hot crusty brown bread made with wholemeal flour, malt, honey, molasses, caraway seeds …

✳

The sound of the night wind singing outside the Abbey with everyone wrapped in silent prayer.

The sound of the sea when you're close enough to the north beach.

The sounds of walking on stones and shells and sand, and how every beach on the island sounds different.

The sound of the pub and, in the music and buzz, someone's laugh you love.

The sound of four-part harmony from the kitchen team.
Teacups on a tray.
Someone crying in service.

✳

The smell of seaweed
composting
into earthy gardens.

The clear, fresh, ozone smell after a rain storm.

The incense of sage and thyme and mint wafting from the Abbey herb garden.

The scent of snow in the air:
the tingle in my nostrils,
leap of my child's heart.

❉

Resurrection moments:

Walking along the Road of the Dead, head and heart heavy with a depression. And suddenly I stop and see all the beautiful little white flowers growing up between the cobblestones. And bend down, feeling love again blooming somehow; feeling the wonder of each precious petal (after days walking around with my head down feeling nothing); the sun coming out (after days of feeling grey). And I look down the road and see all the little moments scattered along it. And the road says life is full of little resurrections. And Jesus says: Look at the birds of the air; they neither sow nor reap yet their heavenly Father feeds them. And the sky says dive into life again.

❉

Moments talking to guests – after service; at tea time. About where they've come from, where they're going.

A guest from the inner city who came to get away from the drink and drugs, and just breathe in the peace and quiet.

An eighty-year-old woman from Hertfordshire who found a plastic bucket and spade down on the north beach, and spent the whole day making sand castles.

'They must have been left there for some reason,' she said and smiled, her life-lined face lit up. Like a little girl's again.

A gentleman from America whom I met in the abbey library one dull day, and got talking to about journeys. (Outside a wintery wind cried and knocked. The library felt intimate and warm.)

We sat down together, and he explained that he had cancer; that he was dying – but that he wasn't afraid any longer. Once you finally accept it he said, you get all you can out of life. Every moment is precious. 'You want to tell everyone you meet that,' he said, and looked at me. He was worried about his friends though, they were all still afraid, and as he quietly, gently spoke I could feel myself opening up to precious life again.

'So, what are you reading?' he asked and smiled.

Do not be afraid, in his eyes.

A retired businessman who came to work and worship.
A busy nurse who came to be still.
A priest who works with refugees on the Texas/Mexico border.
A group from L'Arche.
Teens from Birmingham.
Someone who came alone to see.

The moment when all these different people – women and men, young and old, rich and poor – begin to understand each other; come together like the members of a choir, and the whole Centre sings with an energy; rushes with a spirit.

Moments meeting members of my scattered tribe. People who are trying to live a different way; people who are engaging the powers:

Someone living in a co-op
Someone who is starting an organic food collective
A woman living at Faslane Peace Camp
A man working at L'Arche community.

Moments of not feeling alone in the world.

The grey-haired woman in a fringed and beaded Indian jacket who told me about her three acres and ten cats back in Arizona, and how she opened her home to people with no homes – to refugees, young people, old people, people no one wants …

Moments singing *Fiddler on the Roof* and *Oklahoma!* with a troupe of guests after mealtime. The music and choreography of a chore team working together.

✳

Day off moments: So I run and kick off my shoes to feel the sand and sea between my toes.

Day off moments with no one to call back but oyster-catchers and herring gulls.

Nothing to pick up but messages left in the landscape: How sometimes life is like a thousand shades you could never begin to describe. And sometimes life is simply blue sky, green grass, white waves. And it feels like a fight or swing between the two ways of seeing and being sometimes.

Day off moments with no one to get in touch with but my self again.

No deliveries to pick up but what comes to me, what waves leave at my feet: periwinkles, cowrie shells, pieces of coloured glass like precious stones, willow pattern china.

No details to get lost in but the business of a rock pool.

Nothing to follow up but the path of a shore crab.
Nothing to file but ideas for poems.
No services to attend but the wedding of sea and sky.
Nothing to note but the taste and texture and salty, sharp smell of the day.
No one to meet with but the God of silence and solitude.

Day off moments I retreat into to discover new energy. New energy to take back into work.

✳

Moments working in the shop: The difficult meditation of simple jobs: vacuuming and pricing and making more tea; selling things like Fairtrade coffee , Traidcraft chocolate; friendship bracelets with colours like rainbows and suns, hugs and smiles; books by prophets like Walter Wink, John Pilger, Wendell Berry …

Moments talking to visitors. How some people come into the shop searching for directions to the graves of Danish and Norwegian kings, Macbeth, God, and pillage around for postcards, maps, key chains, then grab the next ferry back; and some people stop to talk:

About their favourite aunt, and how she had the most beautiful, long snow-white hair she'd tie up in red and purple ribbons when she worked in her garden. The craziest hat (they all thought then). About how she used to plant sunflowers between all the rows 'just to keep her vegetables growing happy'.

About how when he goes to the pub he still sometimes asks his father if he'd like a pint too (and he's been dead ten years now come September) and sometimes orders him one anyway and they sit and talk.

About how impossible it is to catch Spirit in a photo or video, and about how the light here is always changing and amazing, and how he walked all the way here from Lindisfarne.

Moments at the till: talking to pilgrims about what they're bringing back with them: hope, energy, a precious moment, a new song to sing …

About what they've come to lay down: anger and resentment, a heaviness. 'The wornoutness of the past,' someone standing at the counter confessed to me. Moments of these trades and exchanges.

✳

The transfigured looks on people's faces when they run in to tell you they saw dolphins in the sound, a seal at Port Ban, puffins on Staffa – a lamb being born.

Moments watching a lamb being born, kicking in its caul, the mother lying panting in the dewy green grass, dark, red blood staining her fleece. Then the pure, bright whiteness … My tears welling up from some place elemental – unforced, natural: the glad feeling of that place strong inside me still (some days I feel no response, walking around worried I could be travelling back to that place of not feeling).

When the little lamb stood finally everybody clapped. Like a burst of light.

✳

Moments when I no longer feel a veil between me and the world. When I take pleasure in the everyday details – details I pass by along the path of a day and seldom notice or pause to appreciate.

- Lichen on rocks and stone crosses.
- The extraordinary play of afternoon light and shadow over the cloisters and over paperwork.
- A far line in the landscape.
- The graceful curve of a neighbour's face
- The tracks of doves in the springtime mud – the prints and creases and claws. The tracks of pilgrims alongside, travelling back and forth from the abbey to the world, searching for peace.

Everyday details I love with a keen, clear love.
A love that wells up as I stand – rooted in the now.

Moments when I feel centred and grounded.

Moments when it doesn't seem crazy, moments when it feels healthy: to love the handle of a gate – its wood polished by waves of pilgrims, smooth as a sea-washed stone; to talk to sheep who answer out of the corners of their mouths; to coo to roosting white doves; to suddenly want to spin round and round under a spray of a million clear bright stars and a comet that makes you want to run burning far into the moonlight deep into the heart of God. Moments when it doesn't seem crazy – to want to feel and live life in all its fullness.

Moments thanking God for everything from
good, simple food to
a gentle breeze to
a shooting star
across
the clear, summer sky

✳

Midnight moments together down on the north beach. Playing tag with the waves and always getting caught. Talking about our childhoods and under-standing friends.

The sand sculpture we made from stones and shells, and how it shone sculpted by moonlight. How we stretched out on the sand together and said prayers to the moon and stars, and walked back in complete silence. The pony we met. And how joy came out like moonlight on the sea. The swim we took.

✳

Moments in the village –
lobster traps and brave,
sea-battered boats with names,
heavy coils of frayed blue rope.
Rubbery cables of seaweed
washed up under a sky that's always changing
(God! how to describe it?
    In the time it takes it has
    changed again,
    elusive as a personality.)
And so I forget about trying and
lay my pen down and
open myself up to its energy.
Close my eyes.

Moments sharing the good news and
comfortable silence.

✳

Moments hiking down to St Columba's Bay and to places with names like
    Little Fairy Meadow
Hill of the Angels
    Plain of the Monks
Little Pat's Pasture
    The Glen of the Temple

Moments tearing up the ordered, bulleted lists I composed on the mainland
and watching them fly free in the wind

Moments noticing heather coming,
juniper, sea holly, wild mountain thyme …

Moments talking to lapwings

Moments at St Columba's Bay

The sea-rounded piece of white marble I picked up there,
and wear round my neck as a talisman against drowning,

against getting caught in an undertow,
against getting sucked down again.

Moments talking with mystic Mario from Chiapas
about drowning in love,
about becoming one with the One

O God, I want to drown in Love

Moments understanding that life is a pilgrimage
and that there is meaning in the search
and that A to B to C is insane

Moments gazing out at the sea and
going with the flow

Moments at the disco feeling the sea
flowing through me

✳

Life in all its fullness. And then, gradually, the feeling of being weighed down again. Of having fallen from grace. Walking around for days like that, heart and head heavy. Until I start to see again: Daffodils coming out – like yellow stars. A dazzling stretch of white sand:

Like God's left a trail of wonder behind to remind dull souls to look up: at the stars, at the heavens. At everything shiny with God.

✳

Evenings in the coffeehouse, sharing stories, music, food; talking passionately about things we care about – world poverty, the environment, justice and peace, living our lives with fullness and purpose and wonder. Dancing together to Nusrat Fateh Ali Khan, The West Coast Ceilidh Band, Fela Kuti, Culture Club:

Henry from Uganda
Astrid from Sweden
Brian from America
Jamal from Pakistan
Peggy from New Zealand
David from Lanark –

Moments when the world is One.

*

Moments meeting pilgrims:

The priest who travelled from Mount Athos.
The woman who came from Alaska.

The beautiful old woman I met on the north beach the other day, sitting on a sand dune with a shopping bag, who told me she'd been trying to get back here for twenty years. 'Heaven, isn't it?' she sighed, watching the waves. And then turned to face the sunset, the red-orange light falling gracefully on her mapped face.

The man I met in the pub one afternoon, who told me he'd been camping alone on Mull and had never felt such peace.

He worked for a big company, he said, and travelled all over the world – Hong Kong, New York, Singapore. 'Know where I was this time last week?' he asked me. 'A strip club in L.A. Know where I was the week before? … Shakespeare in London.' He ordered me a whisky with a nod people noticed, and I went over and joined him.

He sat silent a moment, then began telling me about a woman in his office who had killed herself. She sat a couple desks away; it was busy, but they talked sometimes. No one knew why she did it, they just came in one day and she was gone.

'She was beautiful. Could have had any man she wanted,' he said, and took a drink.

He went camping to get away – bought a tent, one of those camping stoves – to stop, get grounded again. When she killed herself he suddenly became aware of something down inside himself, dying too.

'I just kept seeing her empty desk every place. Know what I mean?' he asked. I nodded.

He gazed out the window; the late afternoon light glowed on the Ross of Mull, on red granite walls and columns; felt like warm touch – on our hands, on our faces. He closed his eyes and told me that he wanted to come back here and stay longer, he had some questions.

'I went into the Abbey church – I'm not religious or anything. But felt something. I said a prayer. Lit a candle.'

Meanwhile, he'd take it around with him, he said – the peace he found, the moment he spent. 'Like a still centre. Glowing down inside yourself. Know what I mean?' he asked. I nodded.

We spoke a little longer; he was dying to tell someone he said. He ordered me another malt whisky; got up and went out on the small talk left. I could see him out the window. Standing, staring out at the sea.

I thought about all he'd told me, and about how much of my time I spend flying around, or sitting closed-up in a corner. Like God was telling me that if I just stopped, just glanced up from me a moment, there was a world of deep experience and communion waiting. People behind newspapers and office desks dying to talk, sunsets ripe as fruit. Life in all its fullness.

I became aware of the choice of every moment: Looking up, or looking down. Reaching out, or folding in. Flying away, or standing firm. Feeling, or unfeeling.

Living or dying.

＊

The spring of machair and the sucking squelch of bog
   High cairns
Low, wet patches of irises
Falling asleep between two hills like in the hollow of God's hand and being woken up by cows.
A path.

No path.

＊

The angry, gassy stink of dry, dead seaweed; sulphury smell of briny pools that sit in themselves. Moments when you can't cover up any longer, hide your self from yourself in a sweetness.

Dark, rainy cold moments. Then the smell of a coal fire calling you back inside the light and laughter.

＊

Moments when the landscape says you are too hard-hearted.
Moments when you finally come to see the sea after all the rocks and hills you've climbed.

Moments when the sky says open up, says if you can't appreciate the beauty and magic and mystery here on this sacred isle what chance do you have back in the 'everyday' world? When the sky says: *Stop and look at me stop and look you are going to die.*

Moments gathering treasure:
oyster shells
    scallops
            periwinkles
    whelks
cowrie shells …

Moments turning colours over and contemplating spirals.

Moments like seashells: Like the tiniest, most perfectly wrought seashell you discover on a walk completely lost to yourself, absorbed instead in the miraculous detail of God's world. Moments you keep wrapped in tissue paper inside a jewellery box. Carry around and take out to remind yourself. Set on a shelf in your room like upon an altar.

Moments like shells and stones you string around your neck and keep close to your heart. To show you've lived; been cradled and tossed; stood on the edge dreaming out. To remind yourself that you are part of God when you feel far away and can't hear or smell the sea. To show you believe in moments.

Moments like a beautiful stone made up of flecks of mica and sunlight, feldspar, red granite, basalt … fished from a wonderful tide-pool moment. Moments like a beautiful stone you carry home in your pocket, and take out to see how it's lost its glistering magic on the way, intensity of wet colour – so you try to recapture it. Shine it with spit and taste the salt. Set it in a glass bowl in tap water.

Moments of holding banners of kelp up for the sunlight to shine through – beautiful as stained glass.

Moments that feel so right: Like a sea-rounded stone in the palm of your hand, perfectly smooth with a good heft.

Moments you carry away with you in your walk. Feeling the good, smooth slide and stretch of bones and joints, feeling comfortable in your skin. Moments your whole body sings. Like a symphony. Like a funk tune.

✳

Moments walking down the road, believing I'm in control, then suddenly getting knocked arse over tea kettle by a good slap of winter wind. Moments of being put in my place. Moments of being picked up like something small and rootless and being thrown six feet!

Moments of floating along with my head in the clouds. Moments of being brought down to earth.

✳

Pub moments:

Sitting ten around a table, buying rounds, sharing crisps. Getting drunk on lager and conversation and wine that makes us glad; the room alight and alive with laughter.

Talking about dreams, plans, families.

Confessing failures, celebrating victories. Praying for health and happiness and true love. Giving thanks to God for friends.

Singing, and raising our glasses to life in all its fullness.

Moments walking home after last orders. The night so still and quiet you can hear the music of the spheres and the sheep in the fields, tugging at the earth.

Moments like a sky full of stars.

Like a tide of jellyfish,
pulsing and drifting on the sea like nebulae.

Late night jamming with Tasmanian Peter and Sweet Jane –
Beatles, Gershwin, Kinks –
then going for cocoa at Joss's all-night kitchen.

Sitting round the coal fire telling our stories as Joss knits – sweaters bright and
warm as her welcome:

About how, when her marriage ended, she bought an old houseboat she
learned to sail and dock, and travelled down all the canals in Great Britain.

Allan talking about his journey:
about how he was a youth worker,
then an engineer,
then a crew member on sailing boats in the Caribbean;
then a Buddhist monk in Thailand.

About how the Buddha led him back to Jesus Christ,
who led him to development work
in a rural village
in Uganda.

Moments talking to friends about
the wonder and mystery of this life.

Moments walking home down the road:

Pink-orange dawns
and the moment the birds start singing

Early morning prayers

The meditation and pleasure of sipping
a good, strong cup of tea.

*

Moments I want, impossibly, to last – and the obvious truth that they do not is the great sadness and joy and challenge of life; the truth I either accept, or keep cushioning and drugging myself against. The truth that makes me love, or cling. Dance, or jump. Cry, or sing. Drink, or drunk. *Will you come and follow me?*

Moments that sustain and strengthen us in sips and pieces.
Moments that change us for ever: born-again moments.

'I've come to see that every moment is a communion,' said a guest here at the final reflection one week.

Neil Paynter

What is the good if Mary gave birth to the Son of God two thousands years ago if I do not give birth to the Son of God today?

We are all meant to be mothers of God – God is always needing to be born.

Meister Eckhart, adapted

For I am sure that neither death, nor life, nor angels, nor principalities, nor things present, nor things to come, nor powers, nor height, nor depth, nor anything else in all creation, will be able to separate us from the love of God in Christ Jesus our Lord.

Romans 8:38–39 (NSRV)

BLESSING

Be strong and courageous;
do not be frightened or dismayed,
for the Lord your God is with you
wherever you go.

Joshua 1:9b (NRSV)

GROW HOPE GROW

Grow hope
Grow
Grow big
Grow strong
Grow kindly

Grow up to the sky
Grow down to earth's core
Grow across the land, the seas
Grow around the world's turning

Grow hope
Grow
Grow bright
Glow clear
Grow gladly

Grow amongst trees
Grow inside cities
Grow between neighbours
Grow within hearts and lives

Grow hope
Grow
Grow now
Grow into tomorrow
Develop, stretch, become
Desire, trust, dream

Go for it hope,
Go grow!

Ruth Burgess

GROWING HOPE

Psalm 9:18	Acts 28:20
Psalm 31:24	Romans 4:18–21
Psalm 33:21–22	Romans 5:1–8
Psalm 39:7	Romans 8
Psalm 42:5–6	Romans 12:12
Psalm 62:5	Romans 15:13
Psalm 71:5	1 Corinthians 13:12–13
Psalm 71:14	2 Corinthians 1:7
Psalm 119:49	2 Corinthians 3:12
Psalm 119:114	Ephesians 1:18–19
Psalm 130:4–7	Ephesians 4:4
Psalm 131:3	Colossians 1:5
Psalm 146:5–6	1 Thessalonians 5:8–9
Proverbs 24:13–14	2 Thessalonians 2:16–17
Isaiah 42:3-4	1 Timothy 1:1
Isaiah 51:5	1 Timothy 4:10
Jeremiah 14:8–9	1 Timothy 5:5
Jeremiah 14:22	1 Timothy 6:17
Jeremiah 17:7–8	Hebrews 3:61
Lamentations 3:21–26	Hebrews 6:10–12
Hosea 2:15	Hebrews 6:18–20
Zechariah 9:12	Hebrews 10:23
Matthew 12:17–21	1 Peter 1:21
Acts 26:6–8	1 John 3:2–3

PRAYER OF THE IONA COMMUNITY

O God, who gave to your servant Columba
the gifts of courage, faith and cheerfulness,
and sent people forth from Iona
to carry the word of your gospel to every creature:
grant, we pray, a like spirit to your church,
even at this present time.
Further in all things the purpose of our community,
that hidden things may be revealed to us,
and new ways found to touch the hearts of all.
May we preserve with each other
sincere charity and peace,
and, if it be your will,
grant that this place of your abiding be continued still
to be a sanctuary and a light.
Through Jesus Christ.
Amen

SOURCES AND ACKNOWLEDGEMENTS

January 1 – 'New ways', by Kathy Galloway, from *The Pattern of Our Days: Liturgies and resources for worship*, edited by Kathy Galloway, Wild Goose Publications, 1996, ISBN 0947988769.

'This is the day' responses © The Iona Community, *Iona Abbey Worship Book*, Wild Goose Publications, 2001, ISBN 1901557502.

January 2 – 'To walk in the light …', by Kathy Galloway, from *Walking in Darkness and Light: Sermons and reflections*, Kathy Galloway, St Andrew Press, Edinburgh, 2001, ISBN 0715207695. Used by permission of Kathy Galloway and St Andrew Press.

January 3 – 'The reawakening to mystery', by Peter Millar, from *This is the Day: Reflections & Meditations from the Iona Community*, Neil Paynter (ed), Wild Goose Publications, 2002, ISBN 1901557634.

'Living with cancer', by Zam Walker, from *Friends and Enemies: A book of short prayers & some ways to write your own*, Ruth Burgess, Wild Goose Publications, 2003, ISBN 1901557782.

'To become aware of the sacramental nature of the cosmos …', by Ron Ferguson, from *Chasing the Wild Goose: The Story of the Iona Community*, Ron Ferguson, Wild Goose Publications, 1998, ISBN 1901557006.

January 4 – 'A prayer for this day', by Tom Gordon, from *A Need for Living: Signposts on the journey of life and beyond*, Tom Gordon, Wild Goose Publications, 2001, ISBN 1901557545.

January 5 – 'Acknowledging our fragility', by Erik Cramb, from *Parables and Patter*, Erik Cramb, Wild Goose Publications (out of print).

January 6 – 'Bless O God, the journey ahead', by Kate McIlhagga, from *The Green Heart of the Snowdrop*, Kate McIlhagga, Wild Goose Publications, 2004, ISBN 1901557855.

January 7 – 'Into the thick of things', by Murphy Davis, from *Hospitality: The newspaper of the Open Door Community*. Used by permission of Murphy Davis. www.opendoor-community.org

January 8 – 'A thread of gold', by J. Philip Newell, from an essay in *Coracle*, the magazine of the Iona Community, www.iona.org.uk

Affirmation from the morning service, Iona Abbey, *Iona Abbey Worship Book*, Wild Goose Publications, 2001, ISBN 1901557502.

January 9 – 'Reborn', by Dr Runa MacKay, from *Exile in Israel: A personal journey with the Palestinians*, Wild Goose Publications, 1995, ISBN 0947988750.

January 10 – 'The fruits of loving', by Scott Blythe, from *Coracle*, the magazine of the Iona Community, www.iona.org.uk

January 11 – 'Qurbani', by Stanley Hope, from an article in *Coracle*, the magazine of the Iona Community, www.iona.org.uk

January 12 – 'I met an Irish woman ...', by Stanley Hope, from an article in *Coracle*, the magazine of the Iona Community, www.iona.org.uk

'O God, I am Mustafah the tailor ...' from Christian Homes of India No 51, taken from *Morning, Noon, Night*, collected and introduced by John Carden, Church Missionary Society, 1976, ISBN 900287268. Also in *the Oxford Book of Prayer*, George Appleton, Oxford University Press, 1985.

January 13 – 'God, thanks for welcoming me again' © Iona Community, from *Iona Community Worship Book* (the black book), Wild Goose Publications, (out of print).

'God welcomes us' responses, by Ruth Burgess, from *Eggs & Ashes: Practical & liturgical resources for Lent and Holy Week*, Ruth Burgess and Chris Polhill, Wild Goose Publications, 2004, ISBN 1901557871.

January 14 – 'Whenever they wanted to escape from others ...', by Ralph Morton, from *Knowing Jesus*, Ralph Morton, published in 1974 by The Saint Andrew Press and The Westminster Press, ISBN 0715202669. Used by permission of The Westminster Press and St Andrew Press.

January 15 – From *Dancing on Slaves*, edited Geoffrey Duncan with Martin Hazell, published by the United Reformed Church, ISBN 0853462364. Used by permission of the URC.

January 16 – Ellen Moxley quote found in *God versus Trident: Constitutional theology in Legal Defence of Ellen Moxley and the 'Greenock three' Peace Women*, Alastair McIntosh.

January 17 – 'Being yourself', by J. Philip Newell, from an essay in *Coracle*, the magazine of the Iona Community, www.iona.org.uk

Responses from the morning service, Iona Abbey, from *Iona Abbey Worship Book*, Wild Goose Publications, 2001, ISBN 1901557502.

January 18 – 'Hope for the world' © 2003 WGRG, Iona Community, Glasgow G2 3DH, Scotland. From the *Iona Abbey Worship Book*, Wild Goose Publications, 2001, ISBN 1901557502. Used by permission of the Wild Goose Resource Group.

January 19 – 'God is on the side of hope' responses, by Ruth Burgess, from *Eggs & Ashes: Practical & liturgical resources for Lent and Holy Week*, Ruth Burgess and Chris Polhill, Wild Goose Publications, 2004, ISBN 1901557871.

Prayer by Kierkegaard © 1956 by The University of Chicago, from *The Prayers of Kierkegaard*, by Perry LeFevre, The University of Chicago Press, ISBN 0226470571. Used by the permission of The University of Chicago Press.

January 20 – Martin Luther King quote, from *Strength to Love*, Martin Luther King. Used by permission of Writers House, New York.

January 21 – 'At the end of this day', by Lynda Wright, from *Bread for the Journey*, Key House, Tabor Trust, 2003. (Key House is a retreat house in Falkland, Scotland, www.keyhouse.org)

January 22 – 'As I dig for wild orchids …', by Izumi Shikibu, from The *Ink Dark Moon: Love poems by Ono no Komachi and Izumi Shikibu, women of the ancient court of Jap an*, translated by Jane Hirshfield, Random House, Inc, 1990, ISBN 0679729585. Used by permission of Random House, Inc.

January 23 – 'I thought that my voyage had come to its end …', by Rabindranath Tagore, from his poem Gitanjali, section XXXV11, originally from *Collected Poems and Plays*, Macmillan, first edition 1936, edition 1985, page 17. From Gitanjali by Rabindranath Tagore, New York: Scribner Poetry/Simon & Schuster, 1997. Used by permission of Simon & Schuster.

January 24 – 'The sacred duty of hospitality', by Alastair McIntosh, from his launch address for Glasgow's Tramway's 'Hidden Garden', 2002. Used by permission of Alastair McIntosh.

January 25 – 'Changing places', by Kathy Galloway, from an article in *Coracle*, the magazine of the Iona Community, www.iona.org.uk

January 28 –Quote from George More from *A Way to God: A biography of George More*, by Mary More, edited by Ron Ferguson, Wild Goose Publications, 1991, ISBN 0947988459.

'Our first task in approaching other people …' – by Canon Max Warren. Used by permission of Church Mission Society.

January 29 – 'Someday we shall dance', by Ed Loring © 2000 The Open Door Community, from *I Hear Hope Banging at my Back Door: Writings from Hospitality*, Ed Loring, The Open Door Community, Atlanta. Used by permission of Ed Loring, www.opendoorcommunity.org 'The Open Door Community is a residential community in the Catholic Worker tradition (we're sometimes called a Protestant Catholic

Worker House!). We seek to dismantle racism, sexism and heterosexism, abolish the death penalty, and create the Beloved Community on Earth through a loving relationship with some of the most neglected and outcast of God's children: the homeless and our sisters and brothers who are in prison.

We serve breakfasts and soup-kitchen lunches, provide showers and changes of clothes, staff a free medical clinic, conduct worship services and meetings for the clarification of thought, and provide a prison ministry, including monthly trips for families to visit loved ones at the Hardwick Prisons in central Georgia. We also advocate on behalf of the oppressed, homeless and prisoners through nonviolent protests, grassroots organisation and the publication of our monthly newspaper, *Hospitality*.' (From the Open Door Community website.)

January 30 – 'What is love if it remains invisible and intangible ...' from *Together on the Way* © 1999 World Council of Churches. Used by permission of Kosuke Koyama and by the World Council of Churches.

February 1 – Viktor Frankl quote from *Man's Search for Meaning*, Viktor Frankl. Used by permission of the Viktor Frankl Institute.

February 2 – 'God dwells among the lowliest of men ...', by Toyohiko Kagawa, from *Meditations*. Meditations by Toyohiko Kagawa copyright 1950 by Harper & Brothers, renewed © 1978 by Sumimoto Kagawa. Used by permission of HarperCollins Publishers.

February 4 – Quote by Hans Küng used by permission of Hans Küng. (See Hans Küng's book *Global Responsibility: In search of a new world ethic*. Also see The Global Ethic Foundation, www.weltethos.org)

February 5 – 'Christian beliefs and values ...', by Larry Nugent, from an article in *Coracle*, the magazine of the Iona Community, www.iona.org.uk

February 7 – 'Prayer of the Russian Christians', translated from French by Rosemary Power. French version from a leaflet by L'Icone de Marie, 89450 Vezelay.

February 8 – 'Christ of every pilgrim path' prayer, by Peter Millar, from *An Iona Prayer Book*, Canterbury Press, 1998, ISBN 1853112054. Used by permission of Peter Millar and SCM-Canterbury Press.

February 9 – 'A welcoming blessing', by Jan Sutch Pickard, from *A Book of Blessings and how to write your own*, Ruth Burgess, Wild Goose Publications, 2001, ISBN 1901557480.

February 10 – 'A garland of flowers', by Stanley Hope, from an article in *Coracle*, the magazine of the Iona Community, www.iona.org.uk

February 12 – Geoff Shaw quote used by permission.

February 13 – Tubby Clayton quote used with permission of Toc H, www.toch.org.uk

February 14 – 'The beginning of love ...', by Thomas Merton, from *No Man is an Island* by Thomas Merton, copyright © 1955 by The Abbey of Our Lady of Gethsemani and renewed by the Trustees of the Merton Legacy Trust. Reprinted by permission of Harcourt, Inc. Also reprinted by permission of Curtis Brown.

Ralph Morton quote, from *Towards Christmas: Bible readings for Advent*, T. Ralph Morton, Iona Community Publishing Department (out of print).

February 15– Ralph Morton quote, from *Towards Christmas: Bible readings for Advent*, T. Ralph Morton, Iona Community Publishing Department (out of print).

February 16 – 'Hope is no half-hearted holy optimism about the far future', by Brian Quail, from 'Resistance and hope rap', in *Trident on Trial: The case for people's disarmament*, Angie Zelter, Luath Press Limited, Edinburgh, 2001, ISBN 1842820044. Used by permission of Brian Quail and Luath Press Limited, www.luath.co.uk

February 17 – 'A community which dances...', by Lesley Orr, from *Wrestling and Resting: Exploring stories of spirituality from Britain and Ireland,* edited by Ruth Harvey, Churches Together in Britain and Ireland, 1999. Used by permission of Lesley Orr and Ruth Harvey.

February 19 – 'I am reminded of the story ...', by Roger Gray, from *Roger: An extraordinary peace campaigner*, Helen Steven, Wild Goose Publications, 1990, ISBN 0947988386.

George McLeod quote from *We Shall Re-Build: The work of the Iona Community on the mainland and on island,* George Macleod, The Iona Community Publishing Department, 1962.

February 20 – 'The spirituality of those who care for the dying ...', by Shelia Cassidy, from *Sharing the Darkness: The spirituality of caring*, Shelia Cassidy, Darton, Longman and Todd, 1988, ISBN 0232 51790 8; Orbis Books, 1992 ISBN 0883447797. Used by permission of Darton, Longman and Todd and by the permission of Orbis Books.

'What people need most is ...', by Tom Gordon, from *A Need for Living: Signposts on the journey of life and beyond*, Tom Gordon, Wild Goose Publications, 2001, ISBN 1901557545.

Dear Joyce letter from *A Need for Living: Signposts on the journey of life and beyond*, Tom Gordon, Wild Goose Publications, 2001, ISBN 1901557545.

February 21 – 'Dancing in the streets', by Ian M Fraser, from *Friends and Enemies: A book of short prayers & some ways to write your own*, Ruth Burgess, Wild Goose Publications, 2003, ISBN 1901557782.

Edith Sitwell extract from the poem Eurydice. Used by permission of David Higham Associates.

February 22 – 'The recurring tragedy of Christian history ...', by Paul Oestreicher, from *The Double Cross,* p.107;108, Darton, Longman & Todd Ltd, 1986, ISBN 0232517053. Used by permission of Paul Oestreicher and Darton, Longman & Todd.

'Forgiving God, we believe that you called us to be salt and light' prayer by Jan Sutch Pickard, from an Agape service, *Iona Abbey Worship Book,* Wild Goose Publications, 2001, ISBN 1901557502.

February 24 – 'Jesus means freedom', by Leith Fisher, from *Will you follow me?: Exploring the Gospel of Mark,* Scottish Christian Press, 2003, ISBN 1904325033. Used by permission of Leith Fisher and St Andrew Press.

February 25 – 'Paradox', by Yvonne Morland, from *Pushing the Boat Out: New poetry,* edited by Kathy Galloway, Wild Goose Publications, ISBN 0947988742.

Bing Xin (Hsieh Ping-hsin) poem included in *A Prayer Treasury,* Lion, 1998, ISBN 0 7459 3993 3. Original source of English translation unknown. Chinese original from the poem Wan Dao (evening prayer) 1, written on May 12, 1922.

February 28 – 'By Christ or any other name ... ' from *The Rock of Doubt,* Sydney Carter, Continuum International Publishing Group, ISBN 0826479677. Reprinted by permission of Continuum International Publishing Group.

March 1 – 'When politics and policies are biased to the poor' responses, by Rachel McCann, from *Holy Ground: Liturgies and worship resources for an engaged spirituality,* Neil Paynter & Helen Boothroyd, Wild Goose Publications, 2005, ISBN 190155788X.

March 2 – 'God is with us' responses © Iona Community, from the Iona Community Members' Book.

March 3 – 'Not counting the women and children', © Kathy Galloway, from a talk.

March 4 – 'Brother, sister let me serve you', by Richard Gillard © copyright 1977 scripture in song (a div of Integrity music Inc)/Sovereign Music UK P.O. Box 356, Leighton Buzzard, LU7 3WP. Reproduced by permission.

March 5 – John Miller quote used by permission of John Miller.

'Can we create safe places ...', by Lesley Orr, from an article in *Echoes* magazine, World Council of Churches. Used by permission of Lesley Orr and the World Council of Churches.

'All are welcome' – by Marty Haugen. Copyright © 1994 by GIA Publications, Inc., Chicago, Illinois. All rights reserved. Used by Permission.

March 6 – 'Regimes depend for their power …', by Helen Steven, from *No Alternative?: Non-violent responses to repressive regimes*, John Lampen (ed.), Michael Bartlett, and Diana Francis, Sessions of York, York, England, UK, 2000, ISBN 1850722439. Used by permission of Helen Steven, John Lampen and Sessions of York.

'Jesus calls us' responses, by Ruth Burgess, from *Eggs & Ashes: Practical & liturgical resources for Lent and Holy Week*, Ruth Burgess and Chris Polhill, Wild Goose Publications, 2004, ISBN 1901557871.

March 7 – 'Seeds of hope', by Kate Compston. Used by permission of Kate Compston, SPCK and Christian Aid. An abridged version of this poem was published in *Bread of Tomorrow*, Janet Morley, SPCK-Christian Aid, 1992.

March 8 – 'A thin black line', by Lesley Orr, from an article in *Echoes* magazine, World Council of Churches. Used by permission of Lesley Orr and the World Council of Churches.

March 9 – 'We alone' from *Horses Make A Landscape Look More Beautiful: Poems by Alice Walker*, copyright © 1984 by Alice Walker, reprinted by permission of Harcourt, Inc, and by David Higham Associates.

March 10 – Ron Ferguson quote from *The Herald*. Reproduced by kind permission of *The Herald* and Ron Ferguson.

March 12 – Ed Loring quote used by permission of Ed Loring.

March 13 –St Francis prayer, from *Iona Abbey Worship Book*, Wild Goose Publications, 2001, ISBN 1901557502.

March 14 – 'So what do you believe in …' by Sydney Carter, from Interview, from *The Two-Way Clock,* Stainer & Bell, London, 1974. Reprinted by kind permission.

March 15 – 'Spectating', by Kathy Galloway, from an article in *Coracle*, the magazine of the Iona Community, www.iona.org.uk

March 16 – 'When I first began working with justice and peace groups …', by Gerard Hughes, from *For God's Sake … Unity: An ecumenical voyage with the Iona Community*, edited by Maxwell Craig, Wild Goose Publications, 1998, ISBN 1901557081. Used by permission of Gerard Hughes.

March 17 – From the hymn 'I bind unto myself today', St Patrick, version by Cecil Frances Alexander, No. 402, Church Hymnary, 3rd Edition, Oxford University Press.

March 19 – 'The Corrymeela Community has for years provided a safe space…', by Kathy Galloway, from an article in *Coracle*, the magazine of the Iona Community, www.iona.org.uk

Extract from the Corrymeela Commitment (which is said at their Service of Dedication) used by permission of the Corrymeela Community, www.corrymeela.org

March 21 – 'Thanksgiving', by Kate McIlhagga, from *The Green Heart of the Snowdrop*, Kate McIlhagga, Wild Goose Publications, 2004, ISBN 1901557855.

March 22 – Joseph Wresinski quote used by permission of ATD Fourth World, www.atd-uk.org

March 24 – 'Doors of hope', by Ian M Fraser, from *Salted with Fire: Life-stories, Meditations, Prayers*, Ian M Fraser, St Andrew Press, 1999, ISBN 0715207628. Used by permission of Ian M Fraser and St Andrew Press.

March 25 – 'The leaders of the world exult in possessing a power …', by Brian Quail, from an article in *Coracle*, the magazine of the Iona Community, www.iona.org.uk

March 26 – 'Enemy of apathy', words John Bell and Graham Maule, © 1988 WGRG, Iona Community, Glasgow G2 3DH, Scotland. From *Enemy of Apathy*, John L. Bell & Graham Maule, Wild Goose Publications, ISBN 0947988270. Used by permission of the Wild Goose Resource Group.

Excerpt from Julian of Norwich, from *Julian of Norwich: Showings*, from The Classics of Western Spirituality, translated from the critical text with an introduction by Edmund Colledge, O.S.A. and James Walsh, S.J., © 1978 by Paulist Press, Inc., New York/Mahwah, N.J. Used with permission. www.paulistpress.com

'All … ah …', by Stanley Hope, from an article in *Coracle* , the magazine of the Iona Community, www.iona.org.uk

March 27 – Statement from Reflection Group 11 at the Council for World Mission Assembly, Ayr, Scotland, 2003 formulated by David Coleman. Used by permission of David Coleman and the Council for World Mission.

March 28 – Rowan Williams, from the foreword to *Sharing God's Planet: A Christian vision for a sustainable future*, Church House Publishing, 2005, ISBN 071514068X. Used by permission of Rowan Williams.

March 29 – 'Singing my blues away', by Kathy Galloway, from *The Love Burning Deep: Poems and lyrics*, Kathy Galloway, SPCK, 1993, ISBN 0281046425. (Out of print) Used by permission of Kathy Galloway.

March 30 – Leonardo Boff, in an interview with Henrike Muller, Jan 27, 2005. WCC Feature. Used by permission of the World Council of Churches.

March 31 – Irish traditional poem translated into English by Rosemary Power.

April 22 – 'To be a creature, one among many …', by Kathy Galloway, from a talk: *Earth, Wind, Fire, Water-God, 2003*. Used by permission of Kathy Galloway.

April 23 – Susan George quote from Dissent Symposium on US Foreign Policy, June 1994. Used by permission of Susan George.

April 24 – 'Between the cracks', by Neil Paynter, from *A Book of Blessings and how to write your own*, Ruth Burgess, Wild Goose Publications, 2001, ISBN 1901557480.

April 25 – From *Sharing in One Hope: Commission on Faith and Order*, Bangalore 1978 (reports and documents from the meeting of the Faith and Order Commission), Faith and Order Paper no. 92, Geneva, Commission on Faith and Order, World Council of Churches, 1978, p.8. Used by permission of the World Council of Churches.

April 26 – 'People do not have to do anything …', by John Austin Baker, from *Travels in Oudamovia*, Faith Press, ISBN 716404354. Used by permission of John Austin Baker.

April 27 – 'Outwitted', by Edwin Markham, from *Poems of Edwin Markham*, selected & arranged by Charles L. Wallis, Harper & Brothers, 1950. Markham Archives of Horrmann Library, Wagner College.

April 28 – Cuban proverb from *Practising the Sacred Art of Listening: A guide to enrich your relationships & kindle your spiritual life,* Kay Lindahl, Wild Goose Publications, 2004, ISBN: 1901557901.

April 30 – 'It can well be argued …', by Leith Fisher, from *Will you follow me?: Exploring the Gospel of Mark*, Scottish Christian Press, 2003, ISBN 1904325033. Used by permission of Leith Fisher and St Andrew Press.

'The task of prophetic ministry is …', by Walter Brueggemann, from *The Prophetic Imagination*, SCM 1978. Used by permission of Walter Brueggemann, SCM-Canterbury Press, and Augsburg Fortress Press.

May 1 – 'A person plays the share markets on the internet or in an office …', by Margaret Legum, from *It doesn't have to be like this: Global economics: a new way forward*, Wild Goose Publications, 2003, ISBN 1901557766. (First published by Ampersand Press, Cape Town, South Africa). Used by permission of Margaret Legum.

'O Christ, the master carpenter' from the *Iona Abbey Worship Book*, Wild Goose Publications, 2001, ISBN 1901557502.

May 2 – 'One of the most exciting aspects of non-violence …', by Helen Steven, from an essay in *Coracle*, the magazine of the Iona Community, www.iona.org.uk

'Anyone involved in non-violence …', by Helen Steven, from an essay in *Coracle*, the magazine of the Iona Community, www.iona.org.uk

'Christ has come to turn the world upside down' responses, by Neil Paynter, from *Iona Abbey Worship Book*, Wild Goose Publications, 2001, ISBN 1901557502.

May 3 – 'Hope growing', by Kate McIlhagga, from *The Green Heart of the Snowdrop*, Kate McIlhagga, Wild Goose Publications, 2004, ISBN 1901557855.

May 4 – 'It is ceremony that makes life bearable …' by George MacKay Brown, from 'The Tarn and the Rosary', in *Hawkfall*, first published by The Hogarth Press, 1974, and also published by Triad/Panther Books, London, 1983, ISBN 0586057706; and in *Hawkfall*, Polygon, 2004, 1904598188. Used by permission of Birlinn/Polygon.

May 5 – 'God of all mercy …', Brother Roger, copyright (c) Ateliers et Presses de Taizé, 71250 Taizé, France. Used by permission of Taizé.

'Lord, let us not dwell in the past', by Richard Moriarty, from *Praying for the Dawn: A resource book for the ministry of healing*, Ruth Burgess & Kathy Galloway, Wild Goose Publications, 2000, ISBN 190155726X.

May 6 – 'Love has no other desire but to fulfil itself …', by Kahil Gibran, from *The Prophet*. Used by permission. Authorisation granted by Gibran National Committee, P.O. Box 116-5375, Beirut, Lebanon; phone & fax: (+961-1) 396916; e-mail: k.gibran@cyberia.net.lb

May 7 – 'the Christian and Jewish scriptures …', by Margaret Legum, from *It Doesn't Have to be Like This: Global economics: a new way forward*, Wild Goose Publications, 2003, ISBN 1901557766. (First published by Ampersand Press, Cape Town, South Africa.) Used by permission of Margaret Legum.

May 8 – 'The teaching of Jesus is that, with him, every year is Jubilee …', by Kathy Galloway, from an article in *Coracle*, the magazine of the Iona Community, www.iona.org.uk

May 9 – Ernest Levy quote used by permission of Ernest Levy.

May 10 – Desmond Tutu quote used by permission of Desmond Tutu.

'Our deepest fear … automatically liberates others', from *A Return to Love* by Marianne Williamson, copyright © 1992 by Marianne Williamson. Reprinted by permission of HarperCollins Publishers and Marianne Williamson.

May 12 – 'Forgiveness, when it happens, is able to remove that dead weight from our past …', by Richard Holloway, from *On Forgiveness,* p. 9, Canongate, 2002, ISBN 184195358X. Used by permission of Richard Holloway and Canongate.

Desmond Tutu quote used by permission of Desmond Tutu. From *No Future Without Forgiveness*, Desmond Tutu, Doubleday, 1999, ISBN 0345496907.

May 13 – Thich Nhat Hanh quote from *Living Buddha, Living Christ*. Used by permission of Thich Nhat Hanh, Plum Village.

May 14 – 'O God, you promise a world …', from *Dear Life: Praying through the year with Christian Aid*, Janet Morley, Hannah Ward and Jennifer Wild (eds) © Christian Aid 1998, ISBN 0904379310. Used by permission of Christian Aid.

May 15 – 'Without taxes, of course, governments would be financially crippled …', by Helen Steven, from *No Alternative?: Non-violent responses to repressive regimes*, John Lampen (ed.), Michael Bartlett, and Diana Francis, Sessions of York, York, England, UK, 2000, ISBN 1850722439. Used by permission of Helen Steven, John Lampen and Sessions of York.

Roger Gray quote from *Roger: An extraordinary peace campaigner*, Helen Steven, Wild Goose Publications, 1990, ISBN 0947988386.

May 16 – Thomas Cullinan quote used by permission of Thomas Cullinan.

May 17 – Excerpt from Helen Cook's letter first published in *Pipeline: The magazine of the Wellspring Community*, August 2003, www.wellspringcommunity.org.au

May 19 – Thomas Merton quote from *Living With Wisdom*, Jim Forest, p. 216, Orbis Books, 1991, ISBN 088344755X. Used by permission of Orbis Books.

May 20 – Fergus Macpherson quote used by permission.

'The priority for the Church …' by George MacLeod, from *The Idea Whose Hour Is Come!*, a pamphlet, 1989.

May 22 – 'At least two species', by Ghillean Prance, from *The Earth Under Threat: A Christian perspective*, Ghillean Prance, Wild Goose Publications, 1996, ISBN 0947988807. Used by permission of Ghillean Prance.

May 23 – Bob Holman quote used by permission of Bob Holman.

'God always takes his stand …', by Karl Barth, from *Church Dogmatics* 11.1, The Doctrine of God, section 30, p. 386, T&T Clark, 1961. Used by permission of T&T Clark/John Knox Press.

'Stand, O stand firm' – From *Many & Great: Songs of the world church, volume 1*, edited & arranged by John L. Bell. Wild Goose Publications, 1990, ISBN 0947988408.

May 24 – 'Anything else we can label or contain', by Ron Ferguson, excerpts from *Grace and Dysentery*, Wild Goose Publications, 1987 (out of print).

May 25 – 'I remember fifteen years ago, when Mandela was still in prison …', by John L Bell, from *Hard Words for Interesting Times: Biblical texts in contemporary contexts*, John L.

Bell, Wild Goose Publications, 2003, ISBN 1901557758. © WGRG 2003. Used by permission of the Wild Goose Resource Group.

'Prayer for Africa' – From *An African Prayerbook* selected by Desmond Tutu, copyright © 1995 by Desmond Tutu. Used by permission of Doubleday, a division of Random House.

May 27 – J.H. Oldham quote from p. 26, *Christianity and the Race Problem*, JH Oldham, SCM Press 1924. Used by permission of SCM-Canterbury Press.

May 28 – 'The new economics', by Margaret Legum, from *It Doesn't Have to be Like This: Global economics: a new way forward*, Wild Goose Publications, 2003, ISBN 1901557766. (First published by Ampersand Press, Cape Town, South Africa.) Used by permission of Margaret Legum.

May 30 – Joseph Wresinski quote used by permission of ATD Fourth World, www.atd-uk.org

June 1 – Quote by Hodding Carter Jr. used by permission of Hodding Carter III.

June 2 – 'We give thanks for our friends …' by Michael Leunig, from *When I Talk To You: A cartoonist talks to God*, Harper Collins, 2004, ISBN 0732280435. Used by permission of Michael Leunig.

June 4 – 'Lord Jesus, it is so wonderful to know of the Spirit which you sent', by George MacLeod, from the prayer 'The spirit which invades our hearts', from *The Whole Earth Shall Cry Glory: Iona prayers*, Wild Goose Publications. © Wild Goose Publications.

June 5 – Excerpt from *Toward the Future* by Pierre Teilhard de Chardin, copyright © 1973 by Edition du Seuil, English translation by Rene Hague copyright © 1975 by William Collins Sons & Co. Ltd. and Harcourt, Inc., reprinted by permission of Harcourt, and by Editions du Seuil.

June 7 – 'Healing service, Iona Abbey', by Robert Davidson, from *Coracle*, the magazine of the Iona Community, www.iona.org.uk

June 9 – 'Separated for God in the world', by Ian M Fraser, from *Celebrating Saints: Augustine, Ninian, Columba*, Reflections 3, Ian M Fraser, Wild Goose Publications, ISBN: 0947988890.

'Dietrich Bonhoeffer talks about the need for "holy worldly" people …', by Ron Ferguson, from *Chasing the Wild Goose: The story of the Iona Community*, Ron Ferguson, 1998, Wild Goose Publications, 1987, ISBN 1901557006.

June 10 – 'Deep peace' blessing, from *Iona Abbey Worship Book*, Wild Goose Publications, 2001, ISBN 1901557502.

June 11 – 'The arms race and the war industry …', by Helen Steven, from an essay in *Coracle*, the magazine of the Iona Community, www.iona.org.uk

'Universal prayer for peace', from *Iona Abbey Worship Book*, Wild Goose Publications, 2001, ISBN 1901557502.

June 12 – Quote from an asylum seeker from Rwanda from Christian Aid. Used by permission of Christian Aid.

June 13 – 'When a silence is broken in the interest of confronting injustices …', © Kathy Galloway, from a talk.

'The violence is IN the silence …', quoted in an article by Lesley Orr, *Echoes* magazine, World Council of Churches, Used by permission of Lesley Orr and by the World Council of Churches.

June 14 – George MacLeod quote from 'The cross' in *Daily Readings with George MacLeod: Founder of the Iona Community*, Ron Ferguson (ed), Wild Goose Publications, 1991, ISBN 1901557553. Originally from *Only One Way Left*. *Only One Way Left* reprinted by Wild Goose Publications in 2005. Print book: ISBN 1905010028/ e-book: ISBN 1905010095.

June 15 – 'give us the grace of gulls …' poem, by Mary Palmer from *Coracle*, the magazine of the Iona Community, www.iona.org.uk

June 16 – Peter Millar quote from *Waymarks: Signposts to discovering God's presence in the world*, Peter Millar, Canterbury Press, 2000, ISBN 1853113360. Used by permission of Peter Millar and SCM-Canterbury Press.

June 20 – 'For genuine asylum-seekers it seems likely to become more difficult …' and prayer, by Stanley Hope, from an article in *Coracle*, the magazine of the Iona Community, www.iona.org.uk

June 21 – 'A story of hope', by Vivienne Davis, from an article in *Coracle*, the magazine of the Iona Community, www.iona.org.uk

June 22 – 'Tears', by Jim Hughes, from *Small Voices*, Jim Hughes, Makar Press, Troon, 2004, ISBN 0954708415.

June 23 – 'Jesus was a loiterer …', by Ewan Aitken, from an article in *Life and Work*. Used by permission of Ewan Aitken and *Life and Work*.

June 24 – 'Community life is there to help us not to flee …', by Jean Vanier, from *The Broken Body*, Darton, Longman and Todd, ISBN 0232517495. Used by permission of Jean Vanier.

July 12 – 'If we could only better recognise …' poem, by Jane Rogers, from *Coracle,* the magazine of the Iona Community, www.iona.org.uk Extract from a longer poem.

July 13 – 'We preach unconditional love in the church …', by Kate McIlhagga, from *In Good Company: Women in the ministry*, Lesley Orr MacDonald (ed), Wild Goose Publications, ISBN 1901557154.

Peter Millar quote from *Waymarks: Signposts to discovering God's presence in the world*, Peter Millar, Canterbury Press, 2000. 1853113360. Used by permission of Peter Millar and SCM-Canterbury Press.

July 15 – Michel Quoist poem from *The Breath of Love*, Michel Quoist, Crossroad Publishing, 1987, ISBN 0824508521. Used by permission of Crossroad Publishing.

'So you begin …' by Mother Teresa, excerpted from *Words to Love by*, by Mother Teresa, text complied and edited by Frank Cunningham. Copyright © 1983 by Ave Maria Press, P.O. Box 428, Notre Dame, IN 46556, www.avemariapress.com Used with permission of the publisher.

July 16 – 'Camas reflection', by Neil Squires, from *Coracle,* the magazine of the Iona Community, www.iona.org.uk Used by permission of Neil Squires.

July 17 – 'The prayer stool', by Graham Kings, first published in *A Touch of Flame: An anthology of contemporary Christian poetry*, Oxford, Lion Publishing, 1989, p. 120. Used by permission of Graham Kings.

July 18 – Bob Holman quote used by permission of Bob Holman.

July 21 – Margaret Mead quote used by permission of the Institute for Intellectual Studies, www.intellectualstudies.org Note: This quote has been registered as a trademark.

'Today I shall dream', by Joy Mead, from *Making Peace in Practice and Poetry*, Joy Mead, Wild Goose Publications, 2004, ISBN 1901557847.

July 23 – 'In the midst of hunger and war' affirmation, Edmund Jones, reproduced by permission of Stainer & Bell, London, England, www.stainer.co.uk

July 24 – Patricia Routledge quote used by permission of Patricia Routledge.

July 26 – 'In my Reformed tradition …', by Ian M Fraser, from *Many Cells, One Body: Stories from small Christian communities*, Ian M Fraser, Risk Book Series, WCC Publications, Geneva, 2003, ISBN 2-8254-1370-4. Used by permission of Ian M Fraser and the World Council of Churches.

'God's people', by Kathy Galloway, from an article in *Coracle,* the magazine of the Iona Community, www.iona.org.uk

July 27 – 'There is a yogic exercise …', by Ruth Harvey, from *In Good Company: Women in the ministry*, Lesley Orr MacDonald (ed), Wild Goose Publications, ISBN 1901557154.

July 28 – 'The truth', by Ron Ferguson, from *Grace and Dysentery*, Ron Ferguson, Wild Goose Publications, 1987 (out of print).

July 29 – Buddhist saying – found in *Peacemaking Day by Day: Daily readings*, Pax Christi, 1990.

July 31 – 'How unlike the North American woodland Indians we are …' by Ghillean Prance, from *The Earth Under Threat: A Christian perspective*, Ghillean Prance, Wild Goose Publications, 1996, ISBN 0947988807. Used by permission of Ghillean Prance.

August 1 – Robert Runcie quote from the 1994 Anglican conference in Colorado, USA.

August 2 – 'Your peaceful presence, giving strength', © Stanbrook Abbey 1974, from *The Stanbrook Abbey Hymnal*. Used by permission of Stanbrook Abbey.

August 3 – 'Following Jesus does not mean clinging …', by Henri Nouwen, from *Jesus: A Gospel*, 2001, Orbis; and from *Seeds of Hope: A Henri Nouwen reader*, p. 166, edited by Robert Durback. Quote used by permission of Random House, Darton, Longman & Todd and the Henri Nouwen Legacy.

August 4 – Jim Wallis quote used by permission of Jim Wallis.

August 6 – 'Children of the atomic age can never forget …', by Leith Fisher, from *Will You Follow Me?: Exploring the Gospel of Mark*, Scottish Christian Press, 2003, ISBN 1904325033. Used by permission of Leith Fisher and St Andrew Press.

'O Sun behind all suns' prayer, J. Philip Newell, from *Each Day & Each Night: A weekly cycle of prayers from Iona in the Celtic tradition*, J. Philip Newell, Wild Goose Publications, 1994, ISBN 094798853X.

August 7 – 'By what power?', by Ruth Harvey, from a sermon. From *Spirituality on the Edge*, 2002. Used by permission of Ruth Harvey.

August 9 – 'There is surely an inherent racism right at the heart …', by Helen Steven, from an article in *Coracle*, the magazine of the Iona Community, www.iona.org.uk

Phil Berrigan quote used by permission of Elizabeth McCalister.

August 10 – 'I want to beg you to be patient towards all that is unsolved in your heart …', from *Letters to a Young Poet* by Rainer Maria Rilke, translated by M.D. Herter Norton. Copyright 1934, 1954 by W.W. Norton & Company, Inc., renewed © 1962, 1982 by M.D. Herter Norton. Used by permission of W.W. Norton & Company, Inc.

August 12 – 'The feeling of solidarity was immense', by Hannah Kenyon, from *Juicy Bits*, the magazine of the youth associates of the Iona Community, www.iona.org.uk

August 13 – 'Solidarity is usually thought of as a political term ...', by Kathy Galloway, from *Solidarity: Another name for love*, Kathy Galloway, Northern Friends Peace Board Pamphlet Series, 1989. Used by permission of Kathy Galloway.

'Most of us recognise ...' by Peter Millar, from *An Iona Prayer Book*, Canterbury Press, 1998, ISBN 1853112054. Used by permission of Peter Millar and SCM-Canterbury Press.

August 14 – 'I remember a conversation I once had with a woman from the Greenham Common Peace Camp ...', by Kathy Galloway, from *Solidarity: Another name for love*, Kathy Galloway, Northern Friends Peace Board Pamphlet Series, 1989. Used by permission of Kathy Galloway.

August 15 – 'As I read these passages from the books of the law ...', by Ghillean Prance, from *The Earth Under Threat: A Christian perspective*, Ghillean Prance, Wild Goose Publications, 1996, ISBN 0947988807. Used by permission of Ghillean Prance.

August 16 – 'Place, belonging and football pitches', by Alastair McIntosh, from *Politics Now*, STV broadcast, 2004. Used by permission of Alastair McIntosh.

August 17 – by Katharine Hankey, from the hymn 'I love to tell the story', *The Methodist Hymnbook*, 1933. Words from Katherine Hankey's poem 'The old, old story'.

August 19 – 'There was a moving story told at Santiago de Compostela ...', by Elizabeth Templeton, from *For God's Sake ... Unity: An ecumenical voyage with the Iona Community*, edited by Maxwell Craig, Wild Goose Publications, 1998, ISBN 1901557081. Used by permission of Elizabeth Templeton.

August 20 – 'A way of life that disregards and damages God's creation ...', from Catholic Bishops of England and Wales, from *The Call of Creation: God's invitation and the human response*, Synod of Bishops, www.catholic-ew.org.uk Used by permission of the Catholic Bishops' Conference of England and Wales.

Prayer by Christopher Irving, from *Celebrating Common Prayer* (Mowbray) © The Society of Saint Francis 1992, is used by permission.

August 21 – 'Almighty God, Creator', from the prayer 'The glory in the grey', from *The Whole Earth Shall Cry Glory: Iona prayers*, George MacLeod, Wild Goose Publications. © Wild Goose Publications.

August 23 – Will D. Campbell quote from *Brother to a Dragonfly*, Will D. Campbell, Continuum, ISBN 0-8264-1268-8. Used by permission of Will D Campbell and Continuum, New York.

George MacLeod extract from the prayer 'A great mystery is your church', from *The Whole Earth Shall Cry Glory: Iona prayers*, George MacLeod, Wild Goose Publications. © Wild Goose Publications.

August 24 – 'Stand first at the foot of the Cross ...', by Mary Levison, from *In Good Company: Women in the ministry*, Lesley Orr MacDonald (ed), Wild Goose Publications, ISBN 1901557154. Used by permission of Mary Levison.

August 25 – 'What I find in the Bible ...', by George MacLeod, from *Daily Readings with George Macleod: Founder of the Iona Community*, Ron Ferguson (ed), Wild Goose Publications, 1991, ISBN 1901557553.

'Christ has no hands but our hands' responses, adapted by Neil Paynter from a prayer attributed to St Teresa of Avila, from *Holy Ground: Liturgies and worship resources for an engaged spirituality*, Neil Paynter & Helen Boothroyd, Wild Goose Publications, 2005, ISBN 190155788X.

August 26 – 'God of the dispossessed ...', by Peter Millar, from *The Surprise of the Sacred: Finding God in unexpected places*, Canterbury Press, 2004, ISBN 1853115940. Used by permission of Peter Millar and SCM-Canterbury Press.

August 27 – 'Celtic blessing' from *Iona Abbey Worship Book*, Wild Goose Publications, 2001, ISBN 1901557502.

August 28 – Alan Boesak quote used by permission of Alan Boesak.

August 29 – 'Credo', by Ruth Burgess, from *Pushing the Boat Out: New poetry*, edited by Kathy Galloway, Wild Goose Publications, ISBN 0947988742.

August 30 – From *Christian Faith and Life*, William Temple, p. 19-20. SCM Press, 1931. Used by permission of SCM-Canterbury Press.

September 3 – 'This is revolution; this is resurrection ...', by Helen Steven, from *Coracle*, the magazine of the Iona Community, www.iona.org.uk

'Forgive us, Lord Jesus, for grain mountains and milk lakes ...', by David Jenkins, from *The United Reformed Church Prayer Book*. Used by permission of David Jenkins.

Quotes from people on Iona, from an article by Jean Young in the Iona Community Report, 2000.

September 6 – 'It was a chilly, overcast day when the horseman spied the little sparrow ...' Source unknown, found in *Peacemaking Day By Day: Daily readings*, Pax Christi, 1990.

September 8 – 'One of the most vital aspects of attempting to discern the truth ...', by Helen Steven, from *No Alternative?: Non-violent responses to repressive regimes*, John

Lampen (ed.), Michael Bartlett, and Diana Francis, Sessions of York, York, England, UK, 2000, ISBN 1850722439. Used by permission of Helen Steven, John Lampen and Sessions of York.

September 10 – 'The issue of demons invites us to face up to the questions …', by Leith Fisher, from *Will You Follow Me?: Exploring the Gospel of Mark*, Scottish Christian Press, 2003, ISBN 1904325033. Used by permission of Leith Fisher and St Andrew Press.

September 11 – Quote from Konrad Raiser used by permission of Konrad Raiser.

'The greatest terrors of this world …', quoted in *Coracle*, the magazine of the Iona Community, www.iona.org.uk

September 13 – 'We pray for peace' responses, by Rosie Miles, from *A Book of Blessings and how to write your own*, Ruth Burgess, Wild Goose Publications, 2001, ISBN 1901557480.

September 14 – 'Hear this true story of an Indian boy …', by George MacLeod, from *The Idea Whose Hour Is Come!*, a pamphlet, 1989.

September 15 – 'About the middle of Ramadan 2000 …', by Stanley Hope, from *Coracle*, the magazine of the Iona Community, www.iona.org.uk

September 16 – 'Don't leave climate change to the experts …' from *The Ecologist* magazine, from 'A false sense of security', an article by Peter Bunyard. Used by permission of *The Ecologist*.

September 17 – 'Jesus Christ is waiting', words John L Bell and Graham Maule © 1988 WGRG, Iona Community, Glasgow G2 3DH, Scotland. From *Enemy of Apathy*, John L. Bell & Graham Maule, Wild Goose Publications, ISBN 0947988270. Used by permission of the Wild Goose Resource Group.

September 18 – Ralph Morton prayer from from *Towards Easter and Beyond*, T. Ralph Morton, Iona Community Publishing Department (out of print).

September 20 – G.K. Chesterton quote used by permission of A.P. Watt Ltd on behalf of The Royal Literary Fund.

September 21 – Prayer from Dominican Peace Action from the *Common Daily Prayer* of Dominican Peace Action. Used by permission of Dominican Peace Action.

September 23 – 'and the Great Spirit who loves us …', by Kathy Galloway, from the poem 'The dream of learning our true name', from *The Dream of Learning Our True Name*, Kathy Galloway, Wild Goose Publications, 2004, ISBN 1901557790.

September 24 – 'As I write, Ramadan is here once again …', by Stanley Hope, from an article in *Coracle*, the magazine of the Iona Community, www.iona.org.uk

September 26 – Extract from Advices and Queries 41, from *Quaker Faith and Practice: the book of Christian discipline of the Yearly Meeting of the Religious Society of Friends (Quakers) in Britain*, 1995. Used by permission of Quaker Books.

'Live simply, so that all may simply live' – St Elizabeth Ann Seton (1774–1821), from a speech in the diocese of Baltimore. These words are also sometimes attributed to Mahatma Gandhi.

September 28 – From *The Rock of Doubt*, Sydney Carter, Continuum International Publishing Group, ISBN 0826479677. Reprinted by permission of Continuum International Publishing Group.

September 29 – Quote from Joyce Gunn Cairns from the catalogue of her *Daughters of Eve* exhibition, which toured in the Scottish highlands and Paris. The catalogue comprises a conversation between Joyce Gunn Cairns and Julie Lawson, Chief Curator at SNPG. Quote used by permission of Joyce Gunn Cairns, www.s-s-a.org/artists/cairns

October 1 – 'The bodies of grown-ups …' poem, by Janet Morley from *All Desires Known*, Janet Morley, SPCK, 1992, ISBN 0281056889. Used by permission of Janet Morley.

'Grandmotherly God', by Richard Sharples, from *Coracle*, the magazine of the Iona Community, www.iona.org.uk

October 3 – From 'This poem' by Elma Mitchell, first published in the collection *People Etcetera* by Elma Mitchell, Peterloo Poets 1987. Used by permission.

October 5 – 'Crossing frontiers', by Ian M Fraser, from *Strange Fire: Life stories and prayers*, Ian M Fraser, Wild Goose Publications, 1994, ISBN 094798867X.

October 6 – 'I will give you a talisman …' from pp.10-11 *Moral and Political Writings of Mahatma Gandhi, Volume 1*, edited by Iyer, Raghavan (1986). Used by permission of Oxford University Press.

October 7 – 'Is not this what our congregational life in the main requires …', by George MacLeod, from *We Shall Re-Build: The work of the Iona Community on the mainland and on island,* George Macleod, The Iona Community Publishing Department, 1962.

October 8 – 'Lord Jesus, it's good to know that you liked in the flesh …', by Kathy Galloway, from *The Pattern of Our Days: Liturgies and resources for worship*, edited by Kathy Galloway, Wild Goose Publications, 1996, ISBN 0947988769.

October 9 – 'An Amerindian has written to me, expressing his anger …' and prayer, by Ian M Fraser, from *Strange Fire: Life stories and prayers*, Ian M Fraser, Wild Goose Publications, 1994, ISBN 094798867X.

October 10 – 'Creating community which is inclusive of people ...', by Yvonne Morland, from an article in *Coracle*, the magazine of the Iona Community, www.iona.org.uk

October 12 – 'Before I visited the Maku Indians on the upper Rio Negro in Brazil ...', by Ghillean Prance, from *The Earth Under Threat: A Christian perspective*, Ghillean Prance, Wild Goose Publications, 1996, ISBN 0947988807. Used by permission of Ghillean Prance.

October 15 – 'A blessing for a work day', by Kate McIlhagga, from *A Book of Blessings and how to write your own*, Ruth Burgess, Wild Goose Publications, 2001, ISBN 1901557480.

October 17 – Joseph Wresinski quote used by permission of ATD Fourth World, www.atd-uk.org

October 19 – RS Thomas poem 'The Kingdom', published by JM Dent, a division of The Orion Publishing Group. Used by permission of the Orion Publishing Group Ltd.

'O God, you have set before us a great hope' prayer, from *Iona Abbey Worship Book*, Wild Goose Publications, 2001, ISBN 1901557502.

October 21 – 'A prayer of thanks for healing love', by Tom Gordon, from *A Need for Living: Signposts on the journey of life and beyond*, Tom Gordon, Wild Goose Publications, 2001, ISBN 1901557545.

October 22 – 'A prayer used in India' from *Morning, Noon, Night*, collected and introduced by John Carden, Church Missionary Society, 1976 ISBN 900287268.

October 23 – Ian Galloway quote from Christian Aid. Used by permission of Ian Galloway.

'In Britain, racism is a denial of our democratic tradition ...', by Stanley Hope, from an article in *Coracle*, the magazine of the Iona Community, www.iona.org.uk

October 24 – 'Treading on the faces of the poor', by George MacLeod, from *The Idea Whose Hour Is Come!*, a pamphlet, 1989.

October 25 – From *Here and Now: Living in the Spirit*, p. 104–105, by Henri Nouwen, The Crossroad Publishing Company, 2002, ISBN 0824519671. Used by permission of The Crossroad Publishing Company.

October 26 – 'Hospitality and generosity', by Alice Kenyon, from an article in *Coracle*, the magazine of the Iona Community, www.iona.org.uk

October 27 – 'A church that doesn't provoke any crisis ...', by Oscar Romero, from *The Violence of Love* (Reading: April 16, 1978), *The Violence of Love*, compiled and translated by James R. Brockman, Orbis Books 2004 ISBN 1570755353. Used by permission of Orbis Books.

October 28 – 'The Bible, corporately presented …', by George MacLeod, from *The Idea Whose Hour Is Come*, a pamphlet, 1989.

'For the word of God in scripture' prayer, from *Iona Abbey Worship Book*, Wild Goose Publications, 2001, ISBN 1901557502.

October 29 – From *Will you follow me?: Exploring the Gospel of Mark*, Leith Fisher, Scottish Christian Press, 2003, ISBN 1904325033. Used by permission of Leith Fisher and St Andrew Press.

October 31 – 'For so many folk in and out of the church …', by Ewan Aitken, from an article in *Life and Work*. Used by permission of Ewan Aitken and *Life and Work*.

November 1 – 'The Saints of God' extract, by Ian M Fraser, from *Candles & Conifers: Resources for All Saints' and Advent*, Ruth Burgess, Wild Goose Publications, ISBN: 1901557960.

November 2 – 'I recently conducted the funeral of a 32-year-old wife and mother who died in our hospice …', by Tom Gordon, from *A Need for Living: Signposts on the journey of life and beyond*, Tom Gordon, Wild Goose Publications, 2001, ISBN 1901557545.

'If it be your holy will', from the prayer 'A veil as thin as gossamer', from *The Whole Earth Shall Cry Glory: Iona prayers*, George MacLeod, Wild Goose Publications. © Wild Goose Publications.

November 3 – 'The courage to say no', by Ron Ferguson, from *Chasing the Wild Goose: The story of the Iona Community*, Ron Ferguson, Wild Goose Publications, 1998, ISBN 1901557006.

'The courage to say yes', by Kathy Galloway, from *Praying for the Dawn: A resource book for the ministry of healing*, Ruth Burgess & Kathy Galloway (eds), Wild Goose Publications, 2000, ISBN 1 901557 26 X.

November 4 – 'Travelling', by David Osborne, from an article in *Coracle*, the magazine of the Iona Community, www.iona.org.uk

November 5 – 'Journey blessing', by Peter Millar, from *Our Hearts Still Sing: Daily readings*, Peter Millar, Wild Goose Publications, 2004, ISBN.

November 6 – 'The more personal we are, the more we have to confront the needs and claims of the community …', by Kathy Galloway, from *Getting Personal: Sermons and meditations*, Kathy Galloway, SPCK, ISBN 0281048479. Used by permission of Kathy Galloway and SPCK.

November 7 – from *An Easter People in a Good Friday World*, John Rackley, Open House Publications, 2003, printed for the Baptist Assembly, Cardiff, 2003.

November 8 – Extract from Advices and Queries 17, from section 1.02 *Quaker Faith and Practice: The book of Christian discipline of the Yearly Meeting of the Religious Society of Friends (Quakers) in Britain*, 1995. Used by permission of Quaker Books.

November 9 – 'Resistance to oppression cannot begin too soon ...', by Helen Steven, from *No Alternative?: Non-violent responses to repressive regimes*, John Lampen (ed.), Michael Bartlett, and Diana Francis, Sessions of York, York, England, UK, 2000, ISBN 1850722439. Used by permission of Helen Steven, John Lampen and Sessions of York. Elias Chacour quote from *Blood Brothers*, Kingsway, 1985.

November 12 – Story by Stanley Hope from an article in *Coracle*, the magazine of the Iona Community, www.iona.org.uk.

November 13 – Joseph Wresinski quote used by permission of ATD Fourth World, www.atd-uk.org

November 14 – 'The essence of sin ...' from *Mud and Stars: A report on the impact of hospice experience on the Church's ministry of healing*, Working Party 1991, Sobell Publications, p.84. Reproduced with permission.

November 15 – 'Perhaps some of this arrogance stems from ...', by Helen Steven, by Helen Steven, from *No Alternative?: Non-violent responses to repressive regimes*, John Lampen (ed.), Michael Bartlett, and Diana Francis, Sessions of York, York, England, UK, 2000, ISBN 1850722439. Used by permission of Helen Steven, John Lampen and Sessions of York.

November 16 – John Miller quote used by permission of John Miller.

November 18 – 'I spent a wonderful day in the House of hospitality ...', by Martin Johnstone, from an article in *Coracle*, the magazine of the Iona Community, www.iona.org.uk

'What the new creation story is telling us today ...', by Matthew Fox, from *Creation Spirituality: Liberating gifts for the peoples of the Earth*, Harper Collins, 1991. Copyright © 1991 by Matthew Fox. Used by permission of HarperCollins Publishers.

November 19 – 'Firas and Itai', by Abi Sampson, from *Juicy Bits*, the magazine of the youth associates of the Iona Community, www.iona.org.uk

November 20 – Daniel Berrigan quote used by permission of Daniel Berrigan.

November 22 – from *The Song of the Bird*, Anthony de Mello, Doubleday, New York, 1982, p. 67-68. Used by permission of Rev. J. Francis Stroud, S.J.

November 23 – 'A world where we look for and find the Spirit at work ...', by Donal Dorr, from *Mission in Today's World*, Columba Press, Dublin, 1990; Orbis Books, Maryknoll, USA. p. 187–188, and p. 16. Used by permission of Donal Dorr, Columba Press and Orbis Books.

November 24 – 'Is it not the essence of prayer ...', by Peter Millar, from *Waymarks: Signposts to discovering God's presence in the world*, Peter Millar, Canterbury Press, 2000. 1853113360. Used by permission of Peter Millar and SCM-Canterbury Press.

November 27 – David Jenkins quote used by permission of David Jenkins.

November 28 – 'I am convinced that self-respect and an acknowledgement of the unique value of every individual is the essence of the gospel ...', by Helen Steven, from *No Alternative?: Non-violent responses to repressive regimes*, John Lampen (ed.), Michael Bartlett, and Diana Francis, Sessions of York, York, England, UK, 2000, ISBN 1850722439. Used by permission of Helen Steven, John Lampen and Sessions of York.

November 29 – 'Stones', by Danus Skene, from *Coracle*, the magazine of the Iona Community, www.iona.org.uk

'Keeping hope alive', © Jan Sutch Pickard, from the collection *Holy Places: Gatherings 2*, by Jan Sutch Pickard, Oystercatcher Press, 2004, ISBN 0954555813.

November 30 – 'Choose life', by Erik Cramb, from an article in *Coracle*, the magazine of ther Iona Community.

December 1 – 'Watch now, dear Lord', St Augustine, from *Iona Abbey Worship Book*, Wild Goose Publications, 2001, ISBN 1901557502.

December 2 – Adapted from a message to the Churches, World Alliance of Reformed Churches Council, Accra 2004, from *Dancing on Slaves*, edited Geoffrey Duncan with Martin Hazell, published by the United Reformed Church, ISBN 0853462364. Used by permission of the URC.

December 3 – Ron Ferguson quote from *The Herald*. Reproduced by kind permission of *The Herald* and Ron Ferguson.

'Carrying a candle', © Jan Sutch Pickard, from *Candles & Conifers: Resources for All Saints' and Advent*, Ruth Burgess, Wild Goose Publications, 2005, ISBN 1901557960.

December 4 – 'We have all known the long loneliness' ... from *The Long Loneliness* by Dorothy Day. Illustrated by Fritiz Eichenberg. Copyright by Harper & Row, Publishers, Inc.; renewed © 1980 by Tamar Teresa Hennessy. Reprinted by permission of HarperCollins Publishers.

December 5 – Dorothee Soelle extract copyright © 1992 by Hoffmann und Campe Verlag, Hamburg. *Es Muss Doch Mehr Als Alles Geben: Nachdenken Über Gott. Theology for Sceptics*, Dorothee Soelle, p. 125, Mowbray, ISBN 0264673336, translation by Joyce

Irwin. Used by permission of Hoffmann Und Campe.

December 6 – 'How can the birth and life of Jesus root us in the life-long struggle to stand with the marginalized …', by Ruth Harvey, from *Coracle*, the magazine of the Iona Community, www.iona.org.uk

December 7 – 'Ideological and psychological control of people's minds and opinions is another of the building blocks of oppression …', by Helen Steven, from *No Alternative?: Non-violent responses to repressive regimes*, John Lampen (ed.), Michael Bartlett, and Diana Francis, Sessions of York, York, England, UK, 2000, ISBN 1850722439. Used by permission of Helen Steven, John Lampen and Sessions of York.

December 8 – 'What is our vision for the future of multiracial Britain? …', by Stanley Hope, from an article in *Coracle*, the magazine of the Iona Community. www.iona.org.uk

December 9 – 'Resist Trident – Celebrate hope', by Brian Quail, from 'Resistance and Hope Rap', in *Trident on Trial: The case for people's disarmament*, Angie Zelter, Luath Press Limited, Edinburgh, 2001, ISBN 1842820044. Used by permission of Brian Quail and Luath Press Limited. www.luath.co.uk.

December 11 – 'One old woman', by Margaret Legum, from *Coracle*, the magazine of the Iona Community. www.iona.org.uk

December 12 – 'If we have Bibles and communion …' by Ian M Fraser, from *Strange Fire: Life stories and prayers*, Ian M Fraser, Wild Goose Publications, 1994, ISBN 094798867X.

December 13 – 'People travel great distances to find holiness …', by Brian Woodcock, from *Advent Readings from Iona*, Brian Woodcock and Jan Sutch Pickard, Wild Goose Publications, 2000, ISBN 190155733.

December 14 – St John of the Cross, from *The Collected Works of St John of the Cross*, translated by Kieran Kavanaugh and Otilio Rodriguez Copyright (c) 1964, 1979, 1991 by Washington Province of Discalced Carmelites ICS Publications, 2131 Lincoln Road, N.E. Washington, DC 20002-1199 U.S.A., www.icspublications.org. Used by permission.

December 15 – Samuel Rayan quote used by permission of Samuel Rayan.

December 16 – 'The gift of making friends', by Stanley Hope, from *Coracle*, the magazine of the Iona Community. www.iona.org.uk

December 17 – 'Faith is entrusting ourselves to this mystery in which we are living …', by Gerard Hughes, from *God, Where Are You?*, Darton, Longman & Todd, 1997, ISBN 023252226X.Used by permission of Gerard Hughes and Darton, Longman & Todd.

December 18 – 'The word 'Now' occurs often in the New Testament …', by Ralph Morton, from *Towards Christmas: Bible readings for Advent*, T. Ralph Morton, Iona Community Publishing department (out of print).

December 19 – Abraham Joshua Heschel quote used by permission of Susannah Heschel and Jacob Neusner.

December 20 – 'George MacLeod is often quoted as saying Iona is a thin place …', by Murphy Davis, from *Hospitality, the newspaper of the Open Door Community*. Used by permission of Murphy Davis, www.opendoorcommunity.org

December 21 – The cost of Trident is equivalent to spending £30,000 a day since the birth of Christ …', by Molly Harvey, from an article in *Coracle*, the magazine of the Iona Community. www.iona.org.uk Used by permission of Molly Harvey.

'Jim Garrison, an American theologian, once told this story …', by Joy Mead, from *Making Peace in Practice and Poetry*, Joy Mead, Wild Goose Publications, 2004, 1901557847.

December 22 – 'One of the most important distinctions I have learned …' by Chief Rabbi Jonathan Sacks, from *The Dignity of Difference: How to avoid the clash of civilisations,* Continuum, London, 2002. Used by permission of Louise Greenberg Books Ltd.

December 23 – 'Night blessing', by Jan Sutch Pickard, from *A Book of Blessings and how to write your own*, Ruth Burgess, Wild Goose Publications, 2001, ISBN 1901557480.

December 24 – 'On Christmas Eve 1993 I was in Nazareth …', by Ewan Aitken, from an article in *Life and Work*. Used by permission of Ewan Aitken and *Life and Work*.

'Christ, be our light' – © 1994, Bernadette Farrell. Published by OCP Publications, 5536 NE Hassalo, Portland, OR 97213. All rights reserved. Used with permission.

December 25 – 'Glory to God in the High St', by George MacLeod, *Daily Readings with George Macleod: Founder of the Iona Community*, Ron Ferguson (ed), Wild Goose Publications, 1991, ISBN 1901557553.

December 26 – 'One survivor of the tsunami …' by Ron Ferguson, from 'Could 2005 Be The Year We Transform Our World?', *The Herald*, 30 Dec, 2004. Reproduced by kind permission of *The Herald* and Ron Ferguson

'A different randomness', from *Tsunami: A personal account*, Rev Erik Cramb.

December 27 – 'Calm brown eyes fixed on me', by Stanley Hope, from an article in *Coracle*, the magazine of the Iona Community, www.iona.org.uk

THE IONA COMMUNITY IS:

- An ecumenical movement of men and women from different walks of life and different traditions in the Christian church
- Committed to the gospel of Jesus Christ, and to following where that leads, even into the unknown
- Engaged together, and with people of good will across the world, in acting, reflecting and praying for justice, peace and the integrity of creation
- Convinced that the inclusive community we seek must be embodied in the community we practise

Together with our staff, we are responsible for:

- Our islands residential centres of Iona Abbey, the MacLeod Centre on Iona, and Camas Adventure Centre on the Ross of Mull

and in Glasgow:

- The administration of the Community
- Our work with young people
- Our publishing house, Wild Goose Publications
- Our association in the revitalising of worship with the Wild Goose Resource Group

The Iona Community was founded in Glasgow in 1938 by George MacLeod, minister, visionary and prophetic witness for peace, in the context of the poverty and despair of the Depression. Its original task of rebuilding the monastic ruins of Iona Abbey became a sign of hopeful rebuilding of community in Scotland and beyond. Today, we are about 250 Members, mostly in Britain, and 1500 Associate Members, with 1400 Friends worldwide. Together and apart, 'we follow the light we have, and pray for more light'.

For information on the Iona Community contact:
The Iona Community, Fourth Floor, Savoy House, 140 Sauchiehall Street,
Glasgow G2 3DH, UK. Phone: 0141 332 6343
e-mail: ionacomm@gla.iona.org.uk; web: www.iona.org.uk

For enquiries about visiting Iona, please contact:
Iona Abbey, Isle of Iona, Argyll PA76 6SN, UK. Phone: 01681 700404
e-mail: ionacomm@iona.org.uk

Wild Goose Publications, the publishing house of the Iona Community established in the Celtic Christian tradition of Saint Columba, produces books, tapes and CDs on:

- holistic spirituality
- social justice
- political and peace issues
- healing
- innovative approaches to worship
- song in worship, including the work of the Wild Goose Resource Group
- material for meditation and reflection

If you would like to find out more about our books, tapes and CDs, please contact us at:

Wild Goose Publications
Fourth Floor, Savoy House
140 Sauchiehall Street,
Glasgow G2 3DH, UK

Tel. +44 (0)141 332 6292
Fax +44 (0)141 332 1090
e-mail: admin@ionabooks.com

or visit our website at
www.ionabooks.com
for details of all our products and online sales